D05B3Z80

Penguin Books

Real Wired Child

Dr Michael Carr-Gregg is one of Australia's highest profile psychologists and an internationally recognised authority on teenage behaviour. He was the founder of the world's first national support group for teenage cancer patients, CanTeen, and has been Executive Director of the New Zealand Drug Foundation, an Associate Professor at the University of Melbourne's Department of Paediatrics, and a political lobbyist. He is currently a consultant psychologist to many schools and national organisations and an official ambassador for the Federal Government's youth suicide prevention programs beyondblue and MindMatters. He has been the resident parenting expert on Channel 7's top-rating Sunrise program since 2005, acts as 'Agony Uncle' for Girlfriend magazine, and has written several books on parenting. He has won many awards for his work.

Real Wired Child

What **parents** need to know about **kids online**

MICHAEL CARR-GREGG

ILLUSTRATIONS BY RON TANDBERG

Penguin Books

PENGUIN BOOKS

Published by the Penguin Group
Penguin Group (Australia)
250 Camberwell Road, Camberwell, Victoria 3124, Australia
(a division of Pearson Australia Group Pty Ltd)
Penguin Group (USA) Inc.
375 Hudson Street, New York, New York 10014, USA
Penguin Group (Canada)
90 Eglinton Avenue East, Suite 700, Toronto, Canada ON M4P 2Y3
(a division of Pearson Penguin Canada Inc.)
Penguin Books Ltd
80 Strand, London WC2R 0RL England
Penguin Ireland
25 St Stephen's Green, Dublin 2, Ireland
(a division of Penguin Books Ltd)
Penguin Books India Pvt Ltd
11 Community Centre, Panchsheel Park, New Delhi – 110 017, India
Penguin Group (NZ)
67 Apollo Drive, Rosedale, North Shore 0632, New Zealand
(a division of Pearson New Zealand Ltd)
Penguin Books (South Africa) (Pty) Ltd
24 Sturdee Avenue, Rosebank, Johannesburg 2196, South Africa

Penguin Books Ltd, Registered Offices: 80 Strand, London, WC2R 0RL, England

First published by Penguin Group (Australia), 2007

1 3 5 7 9 10 8 6 4 2

Design by Karen Trump © Penguin Group (Australia)
Illustrations by Ron Tandberg
Typeset in Simoncini Garamond by Post Pre-press Group, Brisbane, Queensland
Printed and bound in Australia by McPherson's Printing Group, Maryborough, Victoria

National Library of Australia
Cataloguing-in-Publication data:

Carr-Gregg, Michael.
Real wired child : what parents need to know about kids online.

Includes index.
ISBN 978 0 14 300465 3 (pbk.).

1. Internet and children. 2. Internet - Safety Measures. 3. Parenting. I. Title.

004.678083

In memory of Peggy and Kevin O'Connor

Acknowledgements

This is my third book for the lovely people at Penguin and it would not have been possible without the help, support and encouragement of many. Special mention goes to Senior Constable Susan McLean, Victoria's best cybercop, who has unstintingly shared her wisdom, experience and advice and was always quick to answer the late-night emails. I must also extend my thanks to Australia's leading cyber-educator, Robyn Treyvaud, who has been equally generous with her wealth of knowledge and unparalleled understanding of young people and the net. The concept of 'Cyberia' mentioned throughout this book was originally the idea of the enigmatic Jason Clarke from www.mindsatwork.com.au. I am also indebted to Ali Watts and my editor Michael Nolan, whose editorial skills and patience pass all understanding, and to the wonderful Ron Tandberg, who has once again brought my book's key messages to life as no one else could. I'm thankful to my many clients and their families who have allowed me to share their experiences, albeit anonymously, in the pages of this book, in the hope that others may be spared some of their suffering. Last, but certainly not least, my gratitude goes to my beloved family – Therese, Christopher and Rupert – without whom writing this book would have been much harder.

Contents

Foreword by Senior Constable Susan McLean   ix

Foreword by Dr Tim Hawkes   x

Introduction   xiii

Chapter 1: A crash course in the internet   1

Chapter 2: The digital generation gap   11

Chapter 3: What kids do online
                   (and how to help them do it safely)   27

Chapter 4: The dangers   71

Chapter 5: Cyberbullying   89

Chapter 6: Is there such a thing as internet addiction?   121

Chapter 7: Schools and cybersafety   137

Chapter 8: The family internet safety contract   149

Chapter 9: What to say to your kids   167

Resources   175

Index   184

Foreword
by Senior Constable Susan McLean

Real Wired Child contains up-to-date information about what young people are doing online and the potential problems that may be encountered. There can also be serious legal consequences for young people who misuse this technology. It is paramount that parents are aware and involved in their child's online activities. Learn with your child, surf the net together just as you would kick the footy or play in the park, and, if unsure, acquire the knowledge you need to guide and assist your child. Do not bury your head in the sand and hope that it will be okay, or mistakenly believe that 'my child would not do that!' The dangers are real. Your first steps to knowledge and empowerment are in this book.

Senior Constable Susan McLean is a Youth Resource Officer with the Victoria Police

Foreword
by Dr Tim Hawkes

Michael Carr-Gregg has produced another well-written and desperately needed guide for parents – this time for those who want to know what their children are doing online, and what they can do to ensure their children's wellbeing when they venture into cyberspace.

The post-millennial child of the e-revolution has never known a life not dominated by integrated technologies. They will view new software with the same breathless fascination their parents had for V8 engines and multi-functional sewing machines. Children have become 'digital natives' – they operate at twitch-speed in front of visual display units with an ease that is alien to many parents.

Lacking cyberliteracy, some parents wonder what their children are doing and whether their adventures in cyberspace are helping or harming. *Real Wired Child* is a timely book, for it gives help to an adult world that must regain control of those things that are influencing our children. This can be difficult, for many adults do not understand the cyberworld. However, parents can be helped to become 'digital immigrants' who are able to travel to cyberland with their children and journey with them in a responsible fashion to this exciting world of opportunities.

Augmented with a thoughtful range of case studies, Michael Carr-Gregg's book points out the dangers that face children when they engage in online activities. There are pleasures in cyberspace and things that enrich and educate. There are also predators and things that degrade and destroy. *Real Wired Child* gives practical advice to parents on how they might manage their children's communicating, social networking, web surfing, downloading and gaming. More importantly, the book empowers parents in the management of an area of their children's lives which might otherwise do them harm.

Dr Tim Hawkes is Headmaster of The King's School, Parramatta

Introduction

Tony Blair once said that young people were only 13 per cent of the population but 100 per cent of the future. It is self-evident that we depend on our children for our future and, in doing so, we depend on parents to raise these children – to socialise them to become strong, capable citizens; to teach them social values; to protect them from dangers, including those who would exploit or even harm them. Yet it seems that many parents have lost the map and the compass when it comes to parenting their children, especially in the 'wired' world. Too many have raised the white flag in the increasingly intricate and confusing online terrain of Cyberia, where today's children are natives but their parents can be confused foreigners.

This book asks the question, who is raising our kids online? My parents used to fret about TV (sex, violence, antisocial influence and values), while many today worry about the ubiquity of advertising (must-have consumption, junk food), but very few have even begun to get their heads around the impact of the interactive technology which presents all of the above dilemmas and then some, including direct exploitation and harm. Old social problems like fraud, theft and bullying become more complicated and dangerous when they make the transition to the online world. The issue of young people online challenges almost every aspect of our society – psychological, legal, ethical and educational – but many parents aren't the least bit ready for it. It's time to plug in and see what all the fuss is about.

The internet is at the heart of our children's lives. They find it exciting because everything is available and almost anything is possible, but it is dangerous for the same reasons – Cyberia is a frontier without laws, things are not always as they seem, and people are not always who they say they are. The net provides a rich world of education, entertainment and communication, but it can also expose kids to age-inappropriate content and risky social contacts. Today's wired children can and will access whatever's available, whether with innocent curiosity or determination, deliberately or mistakenly, responsibly or rebelliously. They are a generation born with 24/7 access to anyone and anything – our young people are natives in a world to which we are merely visitors, and if you think that world is merely 'virtual', think again. The people and things our kids are playing with are all too real.

The internet is also a world of user-generated content – in other words, the young people using the internet are also actively creating its content. My son can post and receive pictures, stream video, and read and write things visible to anyone online, anywhere in the world. He can also receive unedited, unfiltered information. It is my job to help him think critically about what he posts, reads and sees online, and to steer him clear of illegal activity.

Many of today's parents grew up in the 'stranger danger' days, and we've put much energy into trying to protect our children by isolating them from danger. Don't go wandering off! Don't talk to strangers! Don't trust people you don't know! If they're inside the family home, in their own room, they're safe, right? How ironic then, that with internet access through computers and phones they're wandering off right in front of us, talking to strangers and putting their trust in them.

The fact is, when using text messaging, chatrooms or interactive websites, your child will never know for sure whether the dialogue they are engaging in is with the person they imagine. The internet allows your child and the people they communicate with to become virtual chameleons, creating more identities than David Bowie and Madonna combined, and they rarely have to entertain any notion of responsibility for their actions. Among them, all kinds of adults and children mingle online, but how often do you imagine others have your kid's best interests at heart?

Young people are already there. Nike, Nintendo and Toyota are there. So are advertisers, propagandists, peddlers and paedophiles. On the net, everything is now up for grabs, including our kids, at any age – even 5-year-olds. Right now they're fending for themselves because we've left them alone (and of course they like it that way). Australia has been lucky thus far, but the overseas experience, especially in America, is truly scary. We should learn from it so we don't make the same mistakes. How many parents picking up this book truly know what their children – especially the young ones – were doing online last night? Isn't it time you found out?

How can we protect our kids if we don't really understand where they are? This book is an invitation for all parents to become cyber-anthropologists; to don a virtual pith helmet, backpack and provisions and to venture into the online world of Cyberia, with your children acting as guides. They know their way around, and they have already learnt the special language, customs and mores, so parents can learn from the digital natives who have already explored the structures of cyberspace and built a few of their own.

The key message in this book is: it is time for parents to discover the delights and the dangers of the internet, and, if not to actually become a part of its community, then to at least understand it and get involved.

Part of our job as parents is to butt into our kids' lives even though they want independence. The price you pay is that you might be labelled overprotective at best, and a lousy snooper at worst. It's normal for young people to want privacy, to make new connections with people and to try on different identities – all of which the internet encourages. But it is a parental responsibility to be sure kids know how to be safe and responsible, and within bounds of the law, before letting them loose. It's up to us to make them listen, even though some of our real wired children don't want to hear.

In plain English I've focused on the key five things young people do online – communicating, social networking, web surfing, downloading and gaming – explaining each activity, identifying the risks and advising how parents can minimise them. By the end of the book, you'll understand what's going on, where the dangers lie, how best to approach discussing the issues with your kids, and how to draw up a plan to manage their online experience.

Lest you think I'm exaggerating the dangers of unsupervised online activity, I've included examples throughout the book of real cases I have dealt with in my practice that illustrate the hazards faced by families.

Parents pray this is a passing fad, like yo-yos and hula hoops, but it isn't. Schools think it will be harnessed, but it won't, and governments think it can be restricted, but it can't. Many parents feel they are shut out, on the other side of a bedroom door. It is time to face up to what might be the biggest social issue of our time, one that has the potential to compromise the security of that which is most precious to us – our children.

Chapter 1

A crash course in the internet

If you're among those parents who use the internet regularly, you're probably savvy enough to skip this chapter and start reading about your children's activities. On the other hand, if you're not only internet-challenged but new to computers in the first place – if you don't know a modem from a mouse – you owe it to your online kids to learn the basics. Adult Education Centres and TAFE colleges run courses on computers and the internet, or you could get helpful reference books from your library. The best learning resource might be right in front of you – your wired child can show you round the internet basics.

There's a lot of jargon about computers and the internet, but even understanding a little helps you to have conversations with your kids about them.

What is the internet?

We'll start with the internet, aka 'the net'. The internet is the massive global, publicly accessible network of computers, linked around the world through telephone lines, cables and satellites. It is not owned by any individual, company or state, but its use is regulated by governments in some countries. A 'network of networks', the internet links together millions of smaller domestic, academic, business, and governmental networks, which together provide access to information and services from anywhere in the world with a net connection. Usually, internet connection is a paid service of Internet Service Providers (ISPs), such as Telstra's BigPond, Optusnet or Dodo.

Once connected – 'online' – users have access to common services such as email ('electronic mail', akin to sending a letter), online chat (like a telephone conversation but written) and access to the World Wide Web (more commonly known as 'the web'). The web is the vast collection of documents viewed on websites, which range from informational (such as *The Australian* newspaper's website) to consumerist (Myer's website), and include business, educational and government sites. Websites contain links which, at a mouse-click, open pages within the site or open a new site, allowing viewers to flick rapidly through huge quantities of information and services, the activity known as 'surfing'.

Common methods of home access include dial-up (using a modem); broadband (over phone lines or cable); wireless (Wi-Fi), which connects via cable but transmits throughout the house; satellite; and newer model mobile phones. Public places to use the internet include libraries and internet cafes, with connected computers for hire, as well as terminals in places such as airport halls, coffee shops and hotels. Any computer you see, anywhere, might have an internet connection.

An internet connection enables a person to transmit and receive information, and to share files in the form of text, pictures, movies and sound. There has been a huge change in the way people use the net. In the early days, most users spent their time downloading information, but now the dynamic has changed. People of all ages now more commonly upload information to the web, using the net to express themselves. More and more users, including your kids, are creating the content of the web.

Internet services

The range of internet services changes as new technologies are developed and new ways of using the net grip the public imagination. Here is a quick look at some of today's popular online services.

Web browsing and searching

The most likely starting point for looking at the web is with a browser, a software application that enables you to view and find websites. Websites are located with an address, usually along the lines of 'www.website.com', which is typed into a browser application. Popular browsers include Internet Explorer (Microsoft), Safari (Apple), Netscape, Firefox and Opera. Searching for topics and services for which the website address is unknown is made possible with 'search engine' applications, such as the very popular

Google. Users type in words related to their search interest and are provided with a list of relevant websites. Links contained within websites are used to 'surf' to other relevant sites.

By connecting to the internet, opening a browser and directly visiting websites, or searching with Google for websites relating to a particular interest, people can rapidly access information and services from all over the world, generally unrestricted, and sometimes unreliable and unscrupulous.

Email

Email, short for 'electronic mail', is a service for exchanging written messages online. As with regular postal mail, email requires a unique address, which is usually provided by your ISP when you sign up for an internet connection. Email addresses generally look like 'briansmith@optusnet.com.au', but they don't have to use your real name – usually, you can choose any name you like, enabling online privacy (or secrecy). Email messages are queued in a 'mailbox', to be read by the recipient when they wish. You can also 'attach' files (perhaps images or music) to emails, sending them with your message.

Free email accounts are readily available from certain websites, such as Hotmail, and many people choose to have different
accounts – with different names – which they might use sepa-
rately for work and personal purposes.

Chat

Chat is to email what the telephone is to posting a letter. Chat
opens a channel between two online users to enable instant written message exchanges. Instant messaging (IM) services allow you
to choose 'friends' or 'buddies' – a list of other users with whom
you wish to communicate – and you can have two-way chats with
several others at once. 'Chatrooms' operate more communally,
allowing instant messaging among a group of friends or strangers,
and are often used as online meeting places. Newer technologies
provide a visual representation of the person (known as 'avatars')
and their environment, appearing much like a computer game.
It is also increasingly possible to speak directly through a computer connection with a microphone, bringing chat closer to the

functions of the telephone, and the widespread addition of video cameras ('webcams') allows people to see and hear each other as they communicate. Video links aside, chat identities are chosen and the real person is unseen and unknown. Who anyone is in reality – male or female, friend or foe, of any age – cannot be guaranteed.

Forums

Also known as newsgroups or discussion groups, forums are like a public email list about a specific topic, such as a sport or a TV show. You can send messages which are posted to the forum, and which prompt responses from others, creating an environment of debate and discussion. Some forums are 'moderated', meaning someone is responsible for vetting messages before they are made public to ensure their suitability, but others are completely open.

Social networking

A very popular online activity, especially among young people, is social networking, using services such as MySpace, Xanga and

Facebook. You are provided with a webpage on which to describe yourself and your interests, and perhaps include your picture. You can add a gallery of personal photos, video and music, and update a diary about your life (a 'blog', short for 'web log'). You also include a list of links to your friends' profiles, and can meet new people whose profiles you like and ask to be added to their list. The aim is to accumulate 'friends', and there is enormous social cachet in having a large list.

The appeal of social networking to young people is obvious, and the result is that kids are out there with web pages describing themselves and their friends in what is essentially an adult world. As the risks have become more public, the service providers have sought to provide people with some control over who may see their individual profile. MySpace says they restrict the public areas to people over 18, but my colleague Robyn Treyvaud, a consultant for the Centre for Strategic Education, tells me that many students simply register their age as ninety-nine! Once again, true identity can be easily concealed.

Chapter 2

The digital generation gap

The internet is a public space that's open 24/7 and is as big as the world – in fact, it has no boundaries at all. Parents are dutifully setting up broadband networks in their own homes, oblivious to the fact that they are providing their children with the means to go anywhere. We're standing on the docks waving goodbye as our kids travel to Cyberia, a limitless, mostly lawless land in which we are often clueless foreigners. I write this book in the firm belief that parents need to be made aware of the myriad dangers as their offspring digitally migrate. We need to bridge the digital generation gap, learn about the opportunities and pitfalls, and establish boundaries in Cyberia for our kids, in the form of rules, common-sense behaviour and safe online practices.

Digital natives

American promoter of online education Marc Prensky (www. marcprensky.com) coined the term 'digital natives' to describe today's youth, who have always experienced ubiquitous access to digital media. There is a genuine cultural difference between those of us born before interactive media was so prevalent and those brought up with computers, the internet, hundreds of channels of cable TV, mobile phones, MP3 music players, game consoles and more.

The Australian Bureau of Statistics reported that during the twelve months to April 2003, 1 693 300 young Australians aged 5–14 years accessed the internet. This included 90 per cent of 14-year-olds and 21 per cent of 5-year-olds. Sixty-one per cent of those who accessed the internet at home did so more than once a week, and 14 per cent did so every day. The percentages are sure to be higher now, as is the overall annual figure of child users.

Further, of those participating in daily internet use, 70 per cent were aged 12–14, followed by those aged 9–11 (23 per cent) and 5–8 (7 per cent). My clinical experience leaves me with no doubt that the age group most vulnerable to harassment is that of early adolescence (13–15 years), and we can see that the vast majority of this group is online daily. There are also a lot of kindergarten-aged children wandering around Cyberia.

Our kids, then, are 'digital natives', born with a mouse in their hand. Many parents aren't as comfortable with the online world. Recently, Canada's Media Awareness Network released a report called 'Young Canadians in a Wired World', based on extensive surveys and focus groups. It found that 'for most parents, the technology is a bit like "magic", whereas young people can't imagine what the world must have been like before the technology was available'. It's also interesting that parents thought of the internet negatively and from a very narrow perspective. They said that children are wasting their time chatting and playing games. Don't kids just love to hear that?

If the internet is second nature to today's kids, when should education about online behaviour begin? Well, if British 3-year-old Jack Neal is anything to go by, pretty early is the answer. The

BBC News (25 September 2006) reported online that Jack used his mother's computer to buy a £9000 car on the internet auction site eBay. His parents only discovered their son's successful bid when they received a message from eBay about the soft-top second-hand Barbie-pink Nissan Figaro. Jack's mother had accidentally left her eBay password in her computer and her wired child son pressed the 'buy it now' button. They explained the mistake to the car dealer, who fortunately saw the funny side and said he would re-advertise.

The conclusion one draws from the research is that from a very young age, children will begin exploring the internet, with or without parental supervision. As they get older, they will enjoy greater independence and may be tempted to break the family's internet rules. Innocent curiosity and rebelliousness in children aren't new, but they have different ramifications in the online world.

Why is the internet a unique parenting problem?

There has been an explosion of interactive communications: the internet is the biggest thing since Gutenberg's printing press and it is having a tremendous impact on our society, our institutions and our kids. The Media Awareness Network research found that internet use has become the most significant point of contention between parents and their children.

Young people need boundaries. As I have said in my previous books, the adolescent brain is a work in progress. They are generally not good at impulse control, prioritising or assessing risk, and while internet activities are second nature to them, caution and commonsense are not. What are the aspects of the online life of kids that make it a unique problem for their parents?

Lack of information

This book is necessary because our kids have grown up online and they know way more than we do. They know how to go places and do things we can't, and they know the lingo that sounds to us like a foreign language. They also know how to get around any filters, blocks or history settings we might use to manage where they go online. Despite this digital generation gap, adults have an obligation when they give their child a computer to teach them the appropriate codes of conduct and warn of the potential dangers. This book is about saying to mums and dads we need to fear less and know more.

Portability

The internet gets more transportable every day, which makes it easier for young people to be online more of the time, and away from parental supervision. Whereas today most can go online from a laptop or even a mobile phone, who knows what they'll be using in a year's time! It could be something not yet invented.

Constant change

New websites and services appear and become 'hot' overnight, replacing old favourites. What you teach your offspring about the dangers of one specific site or form of access will be outdated information tomorrow. You may never be up-to-date – even psychologists struggle to keep up with the latest trends. Parents need to focus not just on what are safe and appropriate individual sites, but also on helping their kids learn about safe and appropriate behaviour no matter how and where they go online.

Lack of rules

The majority of young people report that their parents have no rules about their internet use. The result is that there are a lot of real wired children, without supervision, visiting sites, downloading material, creating their own web content, and meeting people and communicating through email, mobile texting, social networking sites and instant messaging (IM). For 90 per cent of teens, home is the main point of internet access, hence it is imperative that parents make clear what is and what is not acceptable.

What kids do and what parents think they do

When NetAlert, the internet safety advisory body set up by the Australian government, teamed with leading online media company ninemsn in late 2005 to provide the first Australian research about parental understanding of their teenage children's online lives, the results were startling. They revealed huge gaps in what parents know about their kids' activities, and an alarming lack of supervision.

For example, a frightening 40 per cent of teenagers might agree to meet in person someone they have 'met' online, and only a paltry 12 per cent would ask their parents for permission first. As you will learn in later chapters, the dangers from your children being enticed to meet strangers are very real.

Perhaps you're suspicious, like 49 per cent of Australian parents surveyed, that your kids might be downloading things without your permission? No wonder – 63 per cent of online teens say they have done so.

Or maybe you think your kids are different, and that their regular home net sessions are spent diligently doing their homework. The NetAlert research showed that while 71 per cent of parents believe their teenage children use the internet for research, a mere 23 per cent of kids say their parents are right.

Of particular concern is that nearly a quarter of teenagers reported that their parents are never around when they're online. The report says over half of home computers are put in a private room, such as an office or bedroom. Monitoring usage is much easier when the family shares a net-connected computer in a public space in the house. The lack of parental supervision is compounded by the increasing popularity of wireless internet connections in homes, allowing for access wherever there is a computer and, in the case of laptops, wherever the user chooses.

This research is supported by similar reports from around the world. A recent study commissioned by a UK child protection technology firm, Crisp Thinking, found that two-thirds of parents made no attempt to monitor their kids' activities. Less than a third limited their kids' online time, or checked the websites they visited and with whom they'd been communicating. Disturbingly, nearly three-quarters of those aged 7–16 said they had passed on their email address, phone number or a picture of themselves to a stranger they have met online.

Clearly, many parents are yet to be convinced of the need to supervise their children's online experiences. Despite the many undoubted benefits of the internet, there are also risks for children of all ages. It is parents' responsibility to ensure their children are provided with ongoing internet safety education.

Case Study

Anne arrived in Year 7 without really having had much interest in the internet, MSN or MySpace. A few of her friends had profiles on Bebo, a social networking website where they could post pictures, write blogs and send messages to one another.

When Anne's school introduced laptops in Year 7, Dad installed a broadband wireless network so she could use her computer in her bedroom. Anne began to spend more and more time in her room – Dad said she was studying, but Mum worried that she was doing less to help around the house and spending too much time on the net socialising.

After a year or so, Anne had become completely preoccupied with the internet. Her thoughts were dominated by what she had done online the day before and what she would do next time she logged on. The moment she got home, Anne felt the need to check her blog, emails and MSN Messenger (to see who was online), and to see what had been posted on her Bebo pages. She was spending increasing amounts of time online in order to achieve life satisfaction and extend her social networks.

Anne's mother pleaded with her to restrict her time online, using a combination of threats, bribery and yelling. In response, Anne tried, but her repeated attempts to control her online habits were unsuccessful. She became restless, depressed and irritable, snapping at everyone and being very oppositional, especially towards Mum. Anne denied there was a problem and lied about the amount of time she spent online.

The family situation began to seriously deteriorate, fuelled by a school report showing a problematic decline in her academic performance. Anne's dad accused her mum of overreacting and she in turn accused him of trivialising a serious problem. Anne began to use her time online as a way of escaping from the growing family problems, and for relieving her feelings of helplessness, guilt, anxiety and depression. Eventually Anne's mum sought professional help as she feared her marriage was in trouble. Anne's internet use was now compromising her educational opportunities and had become a central problem for the entire family.

Anne was dragged unwillingly to a counsellor to whom she initially also lied, but eventually a good rapport was established. She was unable to conceal the extent of her involvement with the internet and she agreed that there was a serious problem. The whole family was educated and their help enlisted.

A major stumbling block was convincing Anne's parents that the net was not inherently evil. Many students starting at a new school check their email, IM and social networking sites as soon as they get home – in many instances they're using the net to build friendships and become accepted at school. Not only do their marks not suffer but, through making new contacts, they can become more socially active and less withdrawn. Their use of the internet is not excessive and overall their use of online communications is positive.

Anne's internet-enabled mobile was replaced with an ordinary phone and she responded well to some cognitive behavioural therapy. The family also employed the use of ENUFF, a computer program which blocked Anne from programs that her parents specified, for a time period that they could set. This was seen as a better way to help Anne self-regulate.

Bringing the digital family together

It is apparent that parents can't afford to remain foreigners in Cyberia while our kids run wild, left to negotiate an adult world on their own. The only choice is to bridge the digital generation gap and get involved in their daily online lives.

We also need to adopt safe family internet practices, as soon as our children are old enough to touch a keyboard. NetAlert has devised free online internet safety educational programs for kids of different age groups: www.nettysworld.com.au for ages 2–7, www.cyberquoll.com.au for ages 8–11, and www.cybernetrix.com.au for those up to eighteen.

Here are some good, basic principles with which to begin:

- From the earliest age, make the internet a family activity. Be involved, spend time online together, and use the experience to teach your children to be safe and responsible online.
- Try to keep the internet-connected computer in a family room, rather than an office or a child's room, so you can supervise its use. Wireless connections can be restricted to specific computers, such as the 'family' one.
- Learn as much as you can about the internet. Review the services your kids want to join to ensure they're suitable. Ask your older kids to show you around the websites and services they like, and to teach you how they work.

- Set clear rules for internet use, with reasonable allowances for young people's needs, interests, and curiosity. Discuss the rules with your kids and monitor their adherence to them. You might choose to write a family internet safety contract and display it near the family computer (see chapter 8).
- Investigate the different parental control tools, blocks and filters available and decide if any are needed for your family. Remember that they can be useful tools, but they can't replace active parental supervision, and the teaching of safe practices and good judgment.

The message is clear – there are more kids online than ever before, and they're online earlier than ever before. Do you know where your kids have been on the net today? If not, read on . . . In the next chapter, we'll look more closely at the key areas of kids' online activity, and consider in what ways parents can provide them with important safety guidelines and set reasonable rules to minimise the dangers.

Chapter 3
What kids do online
(and how to help them do it safely)

Imagine Chloe, 14, coming home from school. After slinging her school bag down in the hallway for people to trip over, she makes a beeline for the kitchen, grabs a handful of cookies and a can of cola, and vanishes into her room. Her bedroom door shuts and her parents don't see her until she is called downstairs for her evening meal. Like hundreds of thousands of parents across Australia, Chloe's parents are blissfully unaware of what is actually transpiring behind her door. They may assume that she is deeply absorbed in reading this year's set text for English, or labouring over a hot Pentium in preparation for tomorrow's French test. Or she may be dutifully completing her homework assignments on the laptop that her school insisted all Year 8 students must have. Of course, wishing to give their children the best opportunities, her parents dutifully installed a wireless network last year, allow-ing her and her siblings, younger sister Amy and older brother John, to have internet access throughout their spacious four-bedroom home.

The truth is that practically anything could be going on behind her door. Wired child Chloe is most likely surfing the net and using social networking sites such as MySpace to stay in touch with a myriad of people – some friends, some new acquaintances and some strangers. She will be using instant messaging programs to chat with friends and may be joining some open discussions on blogs or chatrooms to express her opinions. She might have a window open with some schoolwork on the go too.

Chloe's not doing anything wrong – she's just doing what most normal early adolescents do at the beginning of the 21st century. None of these activities is inherently unhealthy. Some argue that each extends her social skills and may be educational. The problem is that they can equally be used for flirting with anonymous strangers and meeting them in real life, or exploring inappropriate sexual or violent material.

This chapter focuses on the five things Chloe, 8-year-old Amy and 17-year-old John are most likely doing behind their bedroom doors, on the family computer, or even on their phone – communicating, social networking, web surfing, downloading and gaming – explaining the risks and what their parents can and should do to minimise them. We'll start with the key principles that should apply whatever the specific activity – if you can instil these practices in your children from the youngest age, then you're well on the way to helping them safely enjoy the wired world.

Four key online safety principles

1   No personal details

The most important rule is a complete prohibition on revealing personal information online. This means that children must not reveal their real names, date of birth, telephone numbers, postal addresses, school, or anything identifiable, in chatrooms, on forums or in blogs. You should help choose your kids' screen names (or 'usernames'), ensuring they are gender neutral.

2 No meeting strangers

Another critical rule relates to meeting people in real life
who they have met online. Parents have to choose their battle-
grounds and this is one of the most important. You should
absolutely forbid meeting strangers, no matter how friendly or
seemingly trustworthy, no matter how long online communications have proceeded, no matter their avowed age or gender.
It should be a rule that if someone your kids don't know
contacts them, or tries to meet them, they must tell you
straight away.

3 No sharing passwords

Great care must be taken with passwords: they are the only
way your children can protect their online identity. Passwords
should be in place for online services, such as instant messaging, but also to secure use of household computers and laptops
entirely (so the computer cannot be used without the password).
The sharing of passwords, even with closest friends, is a big
no-no. Young children should submit their passwords to their

parents (older children should submit to periodic parental checks on their activities).

4   Agree on time limits and enforce them

Finally, all children need sleep, healthy food and plenty of exercise. Using the internet is not a right, it is a privilege, and if children's internet use interferes with their wellbeing parents must act. Therefore online time limits should be negotiated for each child, as well as clear parameters on what activities are allowed. The limits should be explicitly stated and rigorously policed by parents. The best plan is to negotiate and make rules before the issues arise.

Communicating

Chloe is part of the most tribal generation Australia has ever known, one that sees their friends as their most precious resource. Consequently she will spend a huge amount of time communicating with her tribe, all with mobile phones joined to their hip and computers at home. A 2005 survey by internet company Yahoo! found that 64 per cent of young Australians use instant messaging at least once a day, and a similar survey by ninemsn found that 95 per cent of those aged 12–17 used their popular IM program at least a few times a week.

Chloe, like most teens, took to instant messaging like a duck to water. It's quick and she can talk to four or five people simultaneously. She uses Windows Live Messenger, commonly known by its former name MSN, the free IM program from Microsoft. Activating it opens a window featuring Chloe's list of contacts, a collection of screen names representing other people (they don't use their real names). Some will be part of her peer group, others will be acquaintances and still others will be friends of friends, some of whom she will never have met. Chloe can open an instant messaging session allowing her to chat one-on-one with any of her listed 'friends' who are online. The program also alerts her when other friends go online with their MSN, so she can start individual sessions with them too. Usually, if somebody shows up in her contact list, Chloe's screen name will show up in theirs.

When Chloe's parents walk into her room, like many 14-year-olds she will 'minimise' her buddy list with the click of her mouse, so it can't be seen onscreen. When her parents leave, she will access it again in an instant.

She and her mates spend hours and hours chatting online, glued to the screen. Microsoft and others give them the programs for free because they can be used to target marketing promotions and advertise directly to their young clients. Many parents are unaware of the fact that advertising and marketing are now an inescapable part of using these programs. For example, AOL Time Warner promoted the movie *The Lord of the Rings* by inviting MSN users to 'chat' to an automated system that provided clues to an online competition.

Chatting still generally means written communications, but IM users can also swap files, images and music, play games, and even engage in voice and video chat if the computer has a mic and webcam. The programs have also expanded to allow multi-participant chats.

Chloe might also visit chatrooms, online meeting places where anyone can share instant messages publicly, for the thrill of chatting to strangers, trying on different guises and saying things she'd never say to someone she didn't know in person. She also shares her love of *Desperate Housewives* on a public forum, where fans argue over favourite characters and predict future plot twists.

To help avoid being misunderstood in all this written communication, which can quickly escalate to raging argument, Chloe uses 'emoticons' to depict emotion or tone of voice. They enable her to let someone know whether she's being serious or just joking, and much more. They began as text characters which, when viewed 90 degrees anticlockwise, appear as some variant of a smiley face, like this :) They've evolved into little animated faces, complete with kisses being blown or steam coming out of ears.

While emails are generally stored on the sender's and recipient's computers until deleted, chat is usually considered a more throwaway communication. When Chloe closes the MSN window at the end of the night's IM session, the exchange is gone, unless she deliberately chooses to save it. She may choose to keep a flirty exchange with a boy from school to pore over again later, or a chat that included handy advice on how to get to a party on the weekend. It might also be wise to save threatening or bullying chats, as proof of the exchange for later (see chapter 5). Importantly, anyone else involved in the chat has the option of saving it also, and forums maintain a log of everyone's posts, so things said online can be impossible to retract. Chloe needs to learn that she can't erase anything she says or sends online, and it can all find its way across Cyberia at an alarming speed.

As discussed in *The Princess Bitchface Syndrome* (Penguin 2006), at no other time in Chloe's life is peer group contact so important to her, and this generation's technologies deliver 24-hour connections. Of course, staying connected for young people means having a mobile phone – Chloe's is always switched on and she won't leave home without it. The Yahoo! study found that text messaging (or SMS) was the mobile phone function most commonly used by young Australians. For this, and for online chat, there is a huge lexicon of shorthand – kids in Cyberia have their own language, largely unintelligible to digital immigrants (see box on page 36).

SMS Code Cracker

Here's an introductory guide to the shorthand adopted by adolescents to speed up their online and SMS communications. More complete lists can be found on websites such as NoSlang.com, TeenAngels.org and TeenChatDecoder.com. Alternatively, you could ask your digital native to translate for you.

AFAIK	As far as I know	LOL	Laughing out loud
ASL	Age, sex, location	L8R	Later
ATM	At the moment	MTE	My thoughts exactly
BRB	Be right back	OMG	Oh my God
BFN	Bye for now	OTOH	On the other hand
CUL8R	See you later	PRT	Party
EOL	End of lecture	PRW	Parents are watching
F2F	Face-to-face	ROFL	Rolling on the floor
FWIW	For what it's worth		laughing
G2G	Got to go	TTYL	Talk to you later
GR8	Great	10Q or TY	Thank you
IC	I see	W@	What
IMHO	In my humble opinion	WU	What's up
IOW	In other words	W8	Wait
JAM	Just a minute		

What should parents do about communicating on the net?

- Remember – no personal details online, including photos. Your children should understand that you and their friends know who they are and how to find them, and no one else online needs to.

- Absolutely no meeting people they don't know or new acquaintances made online. Your kids might meet interesting people online but they never know if anyone is who they say they are.

- Children must realise that, armed with their password, someone else can pretend to be them. They should not share their passwords for logging in to IM services, blogs and forums, or for checking email, with anyone other than you. Privacy is an issue, more especially for kids Chloe's or John's age, but as legal guardians parents should be able to inspect the communications of younger kids. That means Amy should set up and share passwords with her parents.

- Young people must be very careful about what they say to other people online, not least because there are some applicable laws.

Everyone should practise good online etiquette. The American safety curriculum program i-SAFE (www.isafe.org) says a great starting point is that if your kids wouldn't say something to someone's face, then they shouldn't say it in IM, or put it in an email or on a blog. The same applies to embarrassing pictures or videos. Cyberbullying is a serious offence, and children must know the boundaries (see chapter 5).

- Ask your children not to respond to any offensive or inappropriate emails and chat, and to show you anything they receive which makes them uncomfortable. Assure them that you understand it's not their fault and that they won't be in trouble with you. Parents must ensure that their children are encouraged to tell them about any problems they encounter online without fear of loss of internet access.

- I-SAFE recommends that agreed time limits should include whether children can use IM or text messages during time meant for homework. Negotiating online time limits for all members of the family can help prevent problems arising from overuse.

Case Study

Brett is a first-year university student who is obsessed with indoor soccer and a rock band called The Naked Aliens. He is a frequent visitor to chatrooms and participates in online discussion groups about The Naked Aliens, joining in debates about their albums, lyrics, styles and influences. As a frequent visitor to the NA chatroom he 'met' and struck up cyber-friendships with quite a few of the regular participants. There was one particular girl he got to know quite well. She seemed really nice and they shared similar views about their favourite band.

Brett even told her about the social soccer team that he played in. After a few more conversations, he shared his email address and they started to communicate on a daily basis. For a while everything appeared fine and normal. Then the tone of their communications seemed to change, and the girl started asking really personal and inappropriate questions. Brett began to feel uncomfortable and realised that she was a little strange, so he made the decision to stop communicating with her.

She peppered him with messages and when he didn't respond she started harassing him, sending him inappropriate emails with seductive photos. When he told her to stop, she sent more abusive messages and even more explicit photos. He contacted his ISP and changed his email address as well as blocking her from sending him any more messages. Despite Brett having blocked direct contact, the girl knew the chatrooms that he liked to visit and she began to post messages on them, making false and abusive statements about him.

After a while, Brett started to get threatening and abusive text messages from an unidentified mobile phone number. The messages said that the sender was going to find him and do terrible things to him. Brett became increasingly distressed and informed his parents, who urged him to report it to the police.

The police discovered that there were various pieces of information about Brett on the net that had helped this girl track Brett down. Brett had a MySpace profile on which he had posted his photo, along with his age, name and suburb, all of which could be viewed by anyone as he had set his profile to be public. Brett's soccer team also had a website that listed when and where his games were each week, and his mobile number had been included as part of the team's contact list. With just a few details that Brett had revealed to this girl about his life, she was able to find out his phone number and where he would be at certain times of the week.

Brett never realised how easy it was for someone to use the net to track a person down in the real world, but after this happened he began to take precautions to protect his identity online. He resolved to try and stay anonymous, and now uses an online name that bears no resemblance to his real name or gender. He also reviewed all the public blogs and websites that he'd uploaded information to, in order to make sure he hadn't revealed any personal information or matched a photo with his real name. Brett learnt that the tiny pieces of information that he had left on the internet could lead to potentially dangerous situations, and that once they were out there, he had no control over where they went.

Social networking

When Chloe gets home from school, she naturally gravitates to where her friends are – cyberspace. Social networking is an important medium in which Chloe and her siblings express themselves, providing a blend of diary, photo album, personal forum and social-standing gauge. Adolescence is fundamentally about a search for identity, emancipation from parents and the desire to be part of a group. Social networking sites provide a fast and effective way to give and receive attention, but not all of it is appropriate.

Chloe's preference is MySpace, probably the best known of hundreds of such sites. By the time you're reading this, a different one may have become the hottest attraction, as literally millions of users readily flock to the newest thing. Chloe's MySpace page, using her screen name 'madgrrl', provides her with a 'presence' on the internet, staking out some space in Cyberia and visibly linking her to her peers.

Her profile includes her age, suburb, likes and dislikes, and photos she's taken (often of herself and occasionally in clothes and poses that her parents would not approve of). Her favourite music plays when visitors view her page, and she provides links to websites she likes, including one for her friend's band and one for a fashion label she favours. Importantly, Chloe's page lists her 'friends', just as IM programs do. These link to MySpace pages of actual friends as well as people she's met online, and permit these people to post messages on her page.

Some social networking sites are completely public, meaning anyone can peruse the sites and anything posted on them. Other sites have various privacy settings, allowing some control over who is provided access to individual profiles. AOL's Red Blog is reputedly one of the most secure, but Chloe's MySpace page allows her to use a 'private' setting. This means no one can access her site unless she accepts their request to be included on her 'friends' list.

Her parents should understand that there is great peer pressure to develop an impressive list of friends. Rather than making her appear discriminating, to have few friends can be seen to reflect a low social status among Chloe's peers. Also, only a certain number of friends can be listed on the front page of Chloe's site, with the others relegated to pages further in. In effect, this can be seen as creating a hierarchy of friends, making social standing and cliques all too tangible.

The content of these sites is generally filtered to reject obscene or otherwise inappropriate material, but some people's profiles undoubtedly contain things Chloe's parents would in all likelihood consider objectionable. They certainly wouldn't want little Amy exposed to it, and she's already interested in setting up a MySpace page like her big sister. Parents must be vigilant, especially with younger children, and should make a point of checking their children's social networking pages.

Chloe's parents should see her site. If it isn't set to 'private', the fact is that anyone can access it at any time, including Mum and Dad, her teachers, her brother, and her enemies. However, it should be 'private' and, if so, her parents will need to ask Chloe to show it to them. If she refuses, they face a few parental choices. First, they can assume the best and drop the subject. Second, they can try to access her site without her permission. Finally, they can assume the worst, and ban her from the computer.

Banning is an inflammatory exercise that is bound to fail – Chloe can find a computer to use at a library, internet café or a friend's house. So, to snoop or not to snoop, that is the question.

After twenty-two years in the business of child and adolescent psychology, my advice is this. If the young person in question is over 15, hangs out with sensible friends, is doing well at school, is civil to her parents and siblings, has a record of being able to be trusted, doesn't have a sensation-seeking temperament and shows no depressive or anxiety symptoms – then parents may elect simply to be vigilant.

If the young person is under 15, or the parents have doubts about their emotional maturity, then they should err on the side of caution and request to see the site. Refusal should be seen as an admission that there is something on the site that the young person does not want their parents to see.

There is a burgeoning business in software enabling parents to spy on their children's online activities (see 'Filters and parental controls', chapter 4). For social networking sites, there are possible means of finding a child's site. The American i-SAFE program (www.isafe.org) gives the following advice to parents who wish to check their children's profiles:

For MySpace, look for the search box. You might try entering your child's name (surrounded by quotation marks for an exact search). But most often they won't use their names. They do, however, often list their schools, so you can check out the school under the groups list. You can also try searching for their friends' names and then scroll down to see if there's a picture of your child on the friend's site. If so, it will appear accompanied by your child's chosen screen name. There will be a name on the picture – that will be your child's website. On Xanga, you can look under blogrings and type in your kid's school. Facebook is harder because access is limited to high school students only. So unless you know a willing student, you're going to have to ask your kid to show you the site.

My preference, rather than doing a James Bond number on young Chloe, would be that her parents simply impress upon her that the private things she posts online just for her friends could potentially be viewed by anyone. Whether or not her profile is set to 'private', she can inadvertently add undesirable strangers to her friends list, giving them access to her site. She also has no control over who can see the posts she makes elsewhere on others' pages. Deleting a post from a site doesn't guarantee that it hasn't already been saved by someone else. It only takes a few posts or emails passed on among friends to rapidly escalate into a message that sweeps across the internet.

A well-known case in point was reported in *The Sydney Morning Herald* (July 2004), about a 17-year-old schoolgirl who was suspended from an exclusive Sydney school when sexually suggestive photographs she'd taken of herself at school in uniform found their way online to some fellow pupils. Via other local schools, the images eventually turned up as far afield as London, and are still passed around online years later.

An area much neglected by parents, schools and the community in general, is Chloe and her friends' education about the legal ramifications of what they do online. Some of what young people do online could set them up for a stretch in juvenile detention. In addition to Commonwealth laws controlling prohibited content and directed to the service providers, there are state and territory criminal laws which apply to everyone who uploads content, including Chloe with her MySpace page. These laws enable prosecution of internet users who make available material that is deemed 'objectionable' or 'unsuitable for minors'. The penalties are serious and apply to anyone over the age of ten.

Another growing area of social networking is virtual communities. These present a visual representation of the participants and an environment, looking much like a computer game. With four million members at the time of writing, and roughly 30 000 logged in at any one time, the current best known and fastest growing virtual world is Second Life. Chloe designed a character to represent her (an 'avatar') and interacts with others in a fantasy digital world that has elements of chat rooms, social networking, gaming and even education and business.

When Chloe logs on to Second Life (SL) as 'madgrrl', she moves her avatar around a world featuring everything from public squares to seaside resorts where she can chat, play, buy, sell and trade with other people. While primarily directed at a more adult audience, it is already gathering a significant young following, despite the offer of the more closely supervised Teen Second Life.

Educational institutions are conducting lectures within virtual classrooms, galleries of digital art and virtual rock concerts attract crowds, and real money changes hands – SL reports millions of US dollars in monthly transactions. Real companies have set up virtual shop here too, with links to real-world purchasing. Commercial enterprise within SL will be huge, providing yet another avenue for marketing, including advertising to children unprotected by adult supervision or regulations.

What should parents do about social networking?

- Banning social networking sites is pointless, so restrict social networking for children around 8-year-old Amy's age to well-protected sites designed for younger users, like Whyville.net and ClubPenguin.com. For teens, put an emphasis on rules and supervision.
- Importantly, ensure all social network sites are set to 'private' or 'friends only'.
- Again – no personal details online. This also means avoiding posts about parties, events, or activities where they could be traced.
- Review all the photos the children are posting. Remember – her profile might be 'private', but Chloe can't control what her friends do with her posts or images. Ask your child

whether she really wants everyone to see what she posts.

- Absolutely no meeting people they don't know or new acquaintances made online.
- Discuss the legal ramifications of what they say and do online.

Web surfing

Like millions of young people across the globe, Chloe, Amy and John log on and surf the web – browsing favourite sites, searching for new ones and following links to sites on all topics imaginable. They do so on the family computer, their wireless laptops, their friends' computers, at internet cafés and increasingly on their mobile phones.

Net connection means children have access to a potentially limitless world of information. Although the majority of Chloe's, John's and Amy's online activities are positive, surfing the web exposes them to a range of commercial messages, privacy invasions, and violent or sexualised content that should raise parental concerns. There's plenty of explicit material that curious minds will come across, deliberately or by chance. And, of course, what might be suitable for John might not be appropriate for Amy.

There are many filtering software options available (see Filters and parental controls, page 80) designed to block a computer's access to certain kinds of websites, but parents must be cautious not to rely solely on filters and so-called 'censorware'. While that might be an attractive option for controlling where Amy goes on the net, Chloe and John can find ways around filters if they want to. They also have ready access when they visit members of the extended family or friends.

Chloe and John also have internet-enabled mobile phones, for which there isn't yet any filtering software. This is significant because the next generation of phones have essentially been designed as miniaturised ultra-portable laptops. The new Apple iPhone, for example, is designed for internet services like email, text messaging and web browsing.

Filter programs will never be substitute for parental

supervision and education. And as the age at which children first access the computer gets younger and younger, education can't start too early. Young Media Australia's president Jane Roberts said in *The Age* (29 July 2006) that children as young as three should be taught internet-safe practices even in child-care centres.

Another nuisance as Amy, Chloe and John roam cyberspace will be their exposure to 'pop-up' advertising. These are windows which open automatically to display advertisements, usually inviting the user to click on them to reveal further details. They might open unwelcome websites and sometimes install viruses, spyware and other programs on your computer, to garner information about your internet use. Most browsers now come with pop-up blockers, which may need to be switched on.

What should parents do about web surfing?

- Supervising the web surfing of children is easiest with the home computer in a central location. Younger kids should not have internet access in their bedrooms. Enforcing that with older kids may be very difficult, so open communication about web browsing is a must.

- Even though they are not perfect, all families should use internet filters, especially for younger children. You should be aware of your ISP's use of filters also.
- If you suspect problematic web browsing, or if agreed family practices are breached (see chapter 8), you might choose to check the history of the browsers to see which sites are being visited. This should be done in the child's presence.
- Ensure your browsers' pop-up blockers are switched on, but there should be a strict rule about never clicking on any pop-ups that somehow get through. Children should also have to ask first before filling out any forms, newsletter subscriptions, contests and the like, which can have similar consequences to pop-ups, or invite spam (unwanted emails containing advertising or scams).

Downloading

Chloe's brother John spends a lot of time downloading all sorts of material, some of it free and some of it requiring payment. There is no shortage of things to buy on the internet, which turns John into a consumer without his leaving the house. Like most internet commerce, paid downloading relies on credit card billing. It is extremely unwise to give your children a credit card, or your credit card numbers, unless you have a yearning to spend your life in penury. Be aware also that if you use the family computer to make online purchases, your credit card details might be saved and set to automatically load on billing pages, which means everyone in the house can use them. (Some online purchases use services such as PayPal, which only require a bank account.)

John begs permission to use his parents' credit card to download music through Apple's iTunes website to put on his iPod portable music player. At the beginning of 2007, Apple announced it had sold more than two billion songs, fifty million television episodes and 1.3 million feature-length films. John also pays to download games, while Chloe wants to buy ringtones for her phone.

The US i-SAFE program makes a point of warning parents to be especially wary of any free downloads. Free downloads are hazardous because they can also install spyware, which checks on your online activity and reports back to the marketers, as well as viruses and worms, malicious software which clogs up computer networks. These unwanted programs can slow your computer's performance dramatically. Such downloads are generally also unrated, meaning your children could get access to unsuitable material.

Of particular concern is the peer-to-peer file sharing of music, videos and games (with programs like BearShare and Limewire) which readily subjects computers to virus attacks. File sharing programs enable you to download a file from someone else's computer, but they are generally a two-way street – other users around the world gain access to the files on your computer in return. And while it may be tempting to download the latest episode of *The Simpsons* or the newest game for free, it is unequivocally illegal to do so.

What should parents do about downloading?

- Explain that peer-to-peer file sharing networks supply illegally copied files – for which steep fines and even jail terms can apply – and that they are common sources of viruses, worms and spyware. It is recommended by i-SAFE that you should delete applications like Limewire, BearShare and BitTorrent from the computer.

- You should have clearly understood guidelines about what family members may and may not download, perhaps as part of a family internet safety contract (see chapter 8).

- I-SAFE says parents need to help children make the connection between a click of a mouse and the subsequent cost. If you permit and pay for legal downloads, you should set limits.

Case Study

Andrew is an inveterate downloader, of music, TV programs, movies, computer programs, screensavers and games. When his dad installed a broadband connection at home, his downloads increased exponentially. In the back of his mind he knew that downloading so much material did pose a security risk, but he didn't think anything really terrible could happen. One day, after he downloaded a new program, he noticed that the computer seemed to be much slower, with web pages taking ages to load, and even writing a Word document or email seemed to take forever. Andrew didn't think too much of it at the time – the family computer was getting old and it had lots of data on it.

But when he next logged on he discovered that his browser's homepage had been changed to a free download site, and when he checked his internet settings he found they had all changed. That wasn't the end of it. Whenever he went online,

Andrew would be bombarded with pop-up advertisements and the computer would crash. Finally, one day he found he couldn't log into his email account, and he discovered that someone was using his address and had tried to access the family's internet banking accounts.

Even though the computer had antivirus software installed, it wasn't picking up anything. What Andrew didn't realise at the time was that when he downloaded the free program, a smaller program had simultaneously downloaded and installed itself somewhere hidden on the computer. It was a spyware program that monitored all the family's internet activity as well as all the key strokes that the family had made while online, including their usernames, passwords and emails. This information was being sent to the spyware developer. Andrew's father took the computer to a specialist who located and removed the spyware, and the family had to contact their bank and ISP to change all their account details.

Andrew and the family learnt that 'free' programs invariably carry a price tag. Part of the family internet safety contract they now have in place stipulates that before any family member downloads anything, they have to ensure that there is no spyware associated with it (there are websites which help locate and destroy such programs), and that the user agreement statements are carefully read.

Online Gaming

All kinds of games are created for computers, from poker to sports simulators to modern warfare strategy games like *Command & Conquer*. These are rated by the Office of Film and Literature Classification in the same way as films, although no R-rating yet exists here. If a game is considered unsuitable for the current maximum restriction of MA15+, it is refused classification, banning it from sale. This was the fate in 2005 of crime thriller *Grand Theft Auto: San Andreas* following the revelation that an explicit sex scene had been hidden in the game. An MA15+

rating was eventually awarded after a modified version was released. In 2005, the game *50 Cent: Bulletproof* was banned for encouraging gang violence and *Marc Ecko's Getting Up: Contents Under Pressure* was banned for encouraging grafitti artists.

Games manufacturers know that the 'edgier' the content the greater the appeal, particularly to young boys like John, which is why they tend to contain sex, violence, obscene language and antisocial behaviour. And the reality is that the more a game provokes an outraged reaction among parents and citizens, the greater its sales.

John particularly likes online games, which connect to huge computer servers and allow him to compete in real-time against others around the world. Of these, the biggest are the MMORPGs – Massively Multiplayer Online Role-Playing Games. These connect hundreds of thousands of players at any one time to play characters in a virtual world. John's favourite is *World of Warcraft*, on which he spends hours each night engaging in a swords-and-sorcery fantasy world to build the fame of his on-screen character, 'DarkThorn'.

Some MMORPGs are free, but most require monthly subscriptions of perhaps $20 and they don't require credit cards for payment. *World of Warcraft* boasted more than eight million subscribers in January 2007. As worlds with the freedom for characters to explore and engage at will, rather than games with ultimate goals, MMORPGs are also unending and tremendously time-consuming.

When John is playing online games, he can also engage in instant messaging chat with other players, and games are often where boys will indulge in IM. Chat means the potential for cyberbullying (see chapter 5), and players who harass others are known as 'griefers'. Of course, John might also join forums to discuss the intricacies of *World of Warcraft* in between sessions (and school).

Some MMORPGs also feature substantial commercial components, selling items of use in the game for real money. There are people who even make a living playing the games expressly to accumulate wealth and special items with their characters, which they then sell to other players for real money.

It is important that parents not demonise games. Many are innocuous, engaging, imaginative fun. There may be other benefits, as described by academics at London's Brunel University who conducted a three-year study of popular MMORPG *RuneScape*. They found that rather than being an antisocial activity, game play (in moderation) could be quite beneficial to players. Dr Simon Bradford and Nic Crowe explained on BBC News online (14 March 2006) that *RuneScape* devotees were adding to their group of friends and developing 'important social and cultural skills which carried significance for real life'. They suggested that rather than demonising such games, parents should recognise that there could be benefits in building friendships and teaching teamwork, as well as developing problem-solving skills.

With the skillful mass media marketing saturation of online gaming manufacturers, especially the big guns of Microsoft and Sony, it is hardly surprising that children of all ages want to go online and want to play online games. But there are a couple of points that need to be borne in mind. First, there is a huge variation in the content of online games – some are innocuous and aimed at young children, such as those included at Club Penguin (www.clubpenguin.com) and Nickelodeon (www.nick.com), while others are more adult and can be insidiously addictive, such as *World of Warcraft*, (www.worldofwarcraft.com) and *RuneScape* (www.runescape.com). The latter games are highly competitive and are structured to reward players who spend vast amounts of time online. Some educational online games have also been developed, such as *Habbo Hotel*, which can build communities and sharpen reading, maths and decision-making skills.

The question of the age at which children should be allowed to start online gaming is as difficult as determining at what age a child can be left at home alone, since all children are different. Age is not an accurate predictor of maturity. The greatest predictor of future behaviour of children is their past behaviour. The only credible response is for all parents to be an expert on their child, to know their individual personality and temperament, and their friends, and to base your decision on an accurate assessment of their capacity to make safe choices.

Senior Constable Susan McLean agrees with my position that no family should allow anyone under 13 to play the adult games, and at 13 to 15 years of age children's game play should be closely monitored.

Once parents have reassured themselves that a game's content is age-appropriate, and that they have safeguarded their children's safety and privacy (ensuring kids use passwords and non-specific screen names), then the biggest remaining threat is that many are highly addictive time-consumers. Parents should set firm limits on the amount of time spent playing games, otherwise they can consume their children's days and nights.

In an ideal situation, access should be limited to no more than an hour a day during the week and no more than two hours a day on the weekend. No gaming should be permitted until homework and household chores have been completed. Online time should be balanced with time spent socialising, playing sport, or engaging in creative pursuits.

Determining rules on kids' game time limits can be particularly difficult when some parents are avid gamers themselves. Children tend to ape what they see, so parents need to model moderation and not allow themselves to fall prey to addictive behaviour.

Games in general are an inescapable part of children's lives: i-SAFE estimates that the time spent playing games, especially online, now rivals the amount of time kids spend watching TV.

While psychologists have failed to reach an agreement on whether a phenomenon of 'internet addiction' actually exists (see chapter 6), in Amsterdam a game addiction clinic was opened in July 2006. According to the clinic, about 20 per cent of gamers could develop a dependency.

What should parents do about online gaming?

- Ensure that the games being played are suitable for the child's age, starting with reference to the Office of Film and Literature Classification.

- Negotiate set time limits for gaming, perhaps as part of a family internet safety contract (see chapter 8), with clearly understood consequences for non-compliance which are immediately and consistently enforced.

- As always, follow rules to protect privacy by not using real names for gaming IDs or anything which reveals personal details.

- Younger children like Amy should not be allowed to use voice chat in games. The others should follow the guidelines for safe chatting, and demonstrate that they know how to block unwanted messages and report offenders to game administrators.

- The same rule applies in online gaming as elsewhere: absolutely no meeting people they don't know or new acquaintances made online.

- If a child persistently refuses to stick to agreed limits, parents might install specialist software programs, such as ENUFF PC, that automatically limit a child's time on the internet, or games and chatting specifically, freeing up time for homework, families or exercise. This also ensures equal time for everyone in a multi-user computer environment. Refer to www.enuffpc.com/documents/homeuse.htm.

Undoubtedly some of the parental action suggested here will prove intensely irritating to older children like Chloe and John, who probably perceive it as a brutal and unwarranted intrusion into their private lives. Regardless, hopefully it represents a first step in the right direction. What Chloe's parents must bear in mind, as discussed in my previous books, is that at 14 their daughter's brain is a work in progress. Research strongly suggests that Chloe's capacity to assess risk, control her impulses and think ahead is only fully developed in her early twenties.

This is why until Chloe grows up, she might have difficulty determining whether a website is good or bad, and may struggle from time to time to determine the future consequences of sending a particular message or clicking on a pop-up. The research is clear that whether we are talking about road safety, alcohol or internet behaviour, supervision and monitoring is essential. Chloe's parents mustn't accompany twenty-first century technology with eighteenth century supervision. The internet is a significant part of our children's lives – we must act to protect and educate them.

Chapter 4
The dangers

There is no doubt that the internet provides educational advantages on a scale never envisaged a generation ago. But as the net evolved from a simple communications tool to globally ubiquitous media, it was inevitable that miscreants would flood in to make mischief. The first official internet harassment report was recorded in 1994 and the number has increased exponentially since then. Not only is misuse of the net on the rise, it seems to be increasingly occurring at an earlier age. According to Senior Constable Susan McLean, a Victoria Police Youth Resource Officer, for every four complaints she gets from secondary schools there is now one from a primary school. For young, immature, inexperienced users, there are significant dangers associated with online activity. Parents need to understand that the potential dangers lie not just in the technology but also in young people's inability to always predict the consequences of their actions.

Australia's most highly publicised case of exploitation using the internet involved a DVD made in the Melbourne suburb of Werribee in 2006, and distributed in part online. An example of the nasty practice known as 'happy slapping' – filming physical attacks for entertainment – the DVD was made by a dozen boys around 18-years-old and features them making chlorine bombs, dropping flares on a homeless man, throwing eggs at taxi drivers and fighting at parties, as well as including press coverage of other incidents. A horrific segment showed the group at Werribee River abusing and assaulting a 17-year-old girl with a mild developmental delay. Some of the boys are seen urinating on the girl, setting her hair on fire, forcing her to participate in sexual activity and throwing her top and jacket into the river. Unbeknownst to her parents, the girl had earlier met a couple of the boys in an online MSN chat session and agreed to meet them at a shopping centre, from where the now twelve-strong group escorted her to the river.

The DVD was packaged as *C**t: The Movie* and a segment entitled 'Pimp My Wife' was posted on the popular online video site YouTube. The perpetrators, who incredibly included their names in 'closing credits', sold DVDs for five dollars at high schools in Melbourne's west, until a *Today Tonight* report led to a police investigation. YouTube removed the segment from its site, amid rumours of a sequel featuring house break-ins, and the boys were suspended from their various schools. At the time of writing eight of the boys have been summonsed to appear in court to face charges of procuring sexual penetration by intimidation, manufacturing child pornography and common law assault.

In response, while announcing a Federal Government scheme to provide families with a free filter package for computers (see below), the Communications Minister Helen Coonan said in *The Age* (25 October 2006) that 'there could be no more glaring an example of how technology is aiding and abetting acts such as these to reach a wider audience at a remarkable pace ... We wouldn't let children ride in a car without a seatbelt or on their bikes without a helmet, so we must ensure they do not go online unprotected'.

The Werribee incident demonstrates the way online life has dramatically increased the potential for bullying and abusive behaviour, in this case through the use of IM chat to initiate the boys' crimes and YouTube to publicise some of them. The potential online availability of such footage also means that any child with a computer can be confronted at any time with material that is both distressing and unsuitable.

What kinds of dangers do young people face?

Predators and personal safety

As the Werribee case so clearly demonstrates, a significant danger associated with the internet is your children's exposure to strangers. There is a great risk of engaging people online who are not who they say they are, and your children can be manipulated into revealing personal details and developing relationships kept secret from friends and family. Ultimately, this can lead to kids being lured to meet predators in real life.

Child pornographers and paedophiles find the internet provides a ready source of potential victims. Usually, early communications between such predators and their victims take place over a long period of time, with the adult pretending to be a child. Over time, they will befriend a child, earning their trust and gathering personal details, as they seek to manipulate the child to engage in sexual activities online or in person. Communication can take place via instant messaging, through blogs and chatrooms, or through social networking sites, and reports suggest online games are attracting predators seeking to engage kids through interaction of their characters within the game.

Inappropriate material

The internet is a window on the world, which means it is full of all the delights and horrors of the human experience. Every time a child goes online they run the risk of viewing material that is unsuitable, frightening, distasteful or illegal. Most parents are aware of the online prevalence of pornography, but children may also come across material that is intolerably violent, gory, hate-filled, prejudiced, propagandist or inflammatory. They may simply be fooled by deliberate misinformation or sensationalism.

Cyberbullying

Cyberspace is a rich stamping ground for bullies, as we'll explore more fully in chapter 5. Teasing, false rumours and threats are all spread through instant messaging, chatrooms, blogs, forums, social networking sites and mobile phone texting. They can be accompanied by embarrassing photographs, which may be doctored to make the desired point. Cyberbullying can cause significant psychological problems for victims, and has even led to suicide.

Financial risks

Increasingly the net has provided unscrupulous people with the chance to trick or defraud others into giving them their money, or access to it. A common scam, known as 'phishing', involves official-looking emails and websites which demand personal information, including passwords or bank account and credit card details. They may appear to be legitimate requests for updates or confirmation from known institutions, such as banks. As a result, financial companies always recommend typing in their websites' addresses to log in, rather than clicking on any links in even official-looking emails.

Elsewhere, there are endless opportunities to spend money online. Widespread commercialism on the net makes it a 24/7 advertising billboard. Educating young people to find their way through this virtual jungle is a crucial part of their online education. Excessive use of subscription services, such as for online games or exclusive website memberships, as well as compulsive shopping on auction sites such as eBay, can all deliver large bills, and young people sometimes have difficulty connecting the mouse click with the financial consequences.

Identity theft

Most parents don't realise that the internet provides amazingly low levels of privacy and confidentiality. Despite the limited protection of software like firewalls and encryption, the only thing standing between your family and a security disaster is a password or a credit card number. An ever-growing number of predators, fraudsters, identity thieves and hackers spend each day dreaming up new scams designed to entice the young and vulnerable to reveal these crucial pieces of personal information.

There is also a risk that revealing personal details can invite unwanted bulk advertising emails (spam) or online predators. Of course, there are legitimate reasons for some sites to request details such as names, email addresses, age, gender and so on, but children should be encouraged to check with parents before ever revealing them.

What can you do if your child is a victim?

Protecting children from sexual exploitation

NetAlert, the Federal Government's internet safety advisory body, advises that any parent who suspects any online child exploitation activity should report it to the Australian Federal Police (AFP) through its Online Child Sex Exploitation Team (OCSET). The AFP states that it is 'responsible for the investigation of online child exploitation including pornography, abuse, grooming and procurement of children. In particular, investigations focus on internet sites carrying exploitative material and operated from an ISP in Australia. Any sites not within Australia are referred to overseas law enforcement agencies.'

If a child is in immediate danger, you should always call 000 or contact your local police. However, NetAlert explains that you can report suspicious behaviour to OCSET directly on (07) 5553 8709 or email national-ocset-omc@afp.gov.au. You might also use online forms at www.afp.gov.au/business/reporting_crime/ reporting_national_crime/online_child_sex_exploitation.

Before making a report, NetAlert suggests gathering as much information as possible, such as the name of the chatroom, website or IM provider, the time and date of the incident, anything known about the alleged offender including their username, and copies of any text of the chat or message that can be obtained. If you need help in making a report, or would like more information, you can contact the NetAlert Helpline by email at enquiries@ netalert.net.au, on their website at www.netalert.net.au/help, or by phone 1800 880 176 (toll free).

Reporting offensive material

Parents who come across potentially illegal material on websites, forums or in downloaded files can report what they have seen to the Australian Communications and Media Authority (ACMA). This body, responsible for the regulation of broadcasting, radio-communications, telecommunications and online content, is part of Australia's scheme to address community concerns about offensive and illegal material on the internet and, in particular, to protect children from exposure to material that is unsuitable for them. The ACMA has online forms for complaints at www.acma.gov.au, and it may direct website hosts to remove prohibited content from their service, advise international authorities to do so, or refer cases to appropriate law enforcement agencies.

Filters and parental controls

No one should underestimate the importance of educating parents about the darker corners of Cyberia and equipping them with the tools to ensure that when their children walk the back streets, they do so safely. Filtering software is designed to control what online material is permitted on a particular computer. It can block access to specific websites or restrict access to a specified set of sites, or the like. The aim of such software is to restrict young people from seeing material which parents and guardians regard as inappropriate.

The latest generation of filters is quite sophisticated, enabling parents to selectively apply filters to web browsing, email, instant messaging and newsgroup activities, or customise restrictions to material related to pornography, drugs, hate and violence, or categories of content which might include tattoos and piercing, gambling, file sharing, and free email services. Programs can now blank out offending words in email or instant messaging applications, and limit online access times by the hour. Some programs offer daily emailed activity reports to the owner, while others allow parents to scan a computer's hard drive for offensive material and a record of visited websites. Many of these filters work covertly, hiding the program on the computer and making it more difficult for children to locate and disable.

In June 2006, the Federal Government announced a National Filter Scheme to provide every Australian family with a free internet filter as part of a $116.6 million package of measures to crack down on internet pornography. At the time of writing, it is planned to supply the filtering software for your home computer by download or a CD-ROM mailed on request. Check with NetAlert on the status of the free filter, on 1800 880 176 or email enquiries@netalert.net.au. All ISPs will also be required to offer filters to new and existing customers at no additional cost.

Naturally, the government's direction that public libraries also install the filtering software ignited a debate within the community. Many council-run libraries say they won't install the filters on the grounds of free speech, arguing that such software can block legitimate and educational sites yet still allow pornographic images. Some filtering companies are hesitant to reveal the lists of sites their software blocks, whilst some parents are unhappy with software that blocks almost everything by default.

But is filtering the answer? The software is notoriously easy to dodge. Many digital natives can download counter-software which can circumvent even the most sophisticated filtering. This was acknowledged recently, when the Victorian Government announced a ban on accessing the video-sharing site YouTube in its 1600 state schools, in a bid to tackle the growing problem of cyberbullying. *The Age* (2 March 2007) reported a student explaining how easy it was to find tips for getting around such restrictions. As with similar attempts to block access to MySpace in schools, the ban will likely prove unenforceable.

Within months of schools around the world instituting such bans and installing blocking software, there is inevitably a proliferation of sites offering free downloads of circumvention software. I have no doubt that a similar campaign will be launched when the Federal Government's new free filter scheme is introduced.

While no filter is foolproof, having a filter is preferable to having nothing. There is a danger that the Federal Government's free filters may lull parents into believing that there is less need for adult supervision. It is often said that the best filter is the one between your child's ears, and combined with education, informed parental supervision and a family internet safety contract, wired children should be able to safely enjoy their time online.

For younger children parents would do well to install the latest filters, but this does not obviate parental responsibility. You still need to monitor and supervise your children while online, and consider drawing up a family internet safety contract to lay down rules (see chapter 8).

Young people need to understand the dangers of their travels in Cyberia. In these days when we talk of the erosion of childhood, as our young people are fast-tracked into adulthood, it may seem counterintuitive to 'scare' our children with stories of cyber-bogymen. However, teaching our children to be suspicious of strangers, cynical about online advertising, sceptical of 'free' offers and other scams is now an essential part of great parenting. Above all, our wired children should grow up with the knowledge that if it seems too good to be true, it always is – especially on the internet.

Case Study

Steve loves online gaming. Almost every day when he comes home from school, and especially on the weekends, he will log on to *World of Warcraft*. Having just started in a new high school some distance from his home, Steve was finding it really difficult to make friends. He was being regularly bullied and having trouble keeping up with the work in his accelerated classes.

He began to play online games more and more and made contact with others who shared his passion for MMORPGs (Massively Multiplayer Online Role-Playing Games). As part of his gaming, Steve would often engage in private conversations with other players through the game's chat facility, discussing game cheats and strategies, or any other topic of interest. It was a way to escape all the stress that emanated from school. Steve's parents became increasingly concerned that he was neglecting his schoolwork, and their nagging became the language of their relationship, further deepening his sense of isolation.

Online, Steve got to know Kevin, who seemed almost as obsessed with *WOW* as he was. Kevin lived in a different city but Steve had finally found someone who seemed to understand him, and they became mates. They began to meet in private chatrooms, and Steve disclosed how sad, depressed and alone he felt. He enjoyed the contact and his mood lifted now that he could 'talk' to someone who truly understood how he was feeling, and respected how he felt about his parents, school and the bullying behaviour of his peers. After a while they exchanged email addresses and mobile phone numbers. When Steve's worried parents shut the computer down or disconnected it from the net, Steve could still text-message Kevin till late at night in the privacy of his bedroom. Kevin started asking Steve some very personal questions but Steve didn't feel uncomfortable, rationalising that they had really become very good friends.

When school holidays started Kevin suggested that they meet. He told Steve that he had asked his mum if Steve could stay over and that she'd not only agreed but offered to buy the plane ticket. Steve thought Kevin's parents must be really cool, especially compared to his – he packed an overnight bag and went to the airport without telling his parents.

When he arrived at the other end, Kevin texted him that they should meet at a particular hotel instead. Steve didn't think it strange, but he never made it to the hotel – he was intercepted by police.

Steve's parents had worked out what had happened and alerted the police. It turned out that Steve's '14-year-old' friend was actually a 44-year-old man. Looking back, Steve now realises that he should never have assumed that Kevin was who he said he was, and that he should have been much more careful about how much personal information he told Kevin about himself. He'd been angry about so many things in his life, he really didn't stop to think about the sort of questions he was being asked and why someone might show extra interest in him.

Chapter 5
Cyberbullying

For a 12-year-old girl in the little town of Putaruru (population 3765), on New Zealand's North Island, school became a nightmare, until she could take no more. *The New Zealand Herald* (11 March 2006) reported that the day before school started in 2006 Alex Teka was found dead, having cut her wrists and bled to death in the back garden of her home.

For some seven months, Alex had been bullied in what her mother Deanne described as 'an orchestrated campaign by email and text', conducted by a group of slightly older girls. Deanne told the newspaper the girls accused Alex of abusing one of their sisters, and their revenge escalated to a threat against her life. Deanne said she believes her daughter was a victim of 'tall poppy syndrome'.

There had been signs of a problem earlier the previous year when Alex said she was ill and stayed home from school. At home more than a week, she finally confessed the problem to her mother and showed her the messages. They included physical threats and taunts such as, 'You better not come to school because nobody likes you'.

When Alex's mum told the school, they offered to let Alex choose a different class, but the bullying continued. The *Herald* said 'the school contacted the parents of the identified bullies, discussed bullying at assembly, and put out a newsletter to parents', but Deanne felt that this served to make things worse by making Alex appear to be 'a nark'.

More threats followed over the Christmas holidays, including taunts that Alex's boyfriend was cheating on her. While her mum told the *Herald* she thought Alex's problems 'were likely to be more complicated than just bullying', she said 'the abuse played a major role in her unhappiness'.

The end result was that 'a vibrant and sporty young girl . . . known for singing loudly around the house' took her own life.

Sadly, Alex's story is not as unusual as one may think. The

authorities clearly identified her as a victim of cyberbullying, until recently dismissed as alarmist claptrap by elements of the gutter press. But the reality is that the new generation of bullies is taking their torture to a new level in cyberspace, using email, instant messaging, online diaries, websites, and web forums to harass, humiliate, intimidate and threaten other young people. It is a phenomenon that has become so acute that the stress is leading to some adolescents, like Alex, withdrawing socially, dropping out of school, and in some cases, tragically choosing to end their lives.

While many parents justifiably worry about technology in the hands of perverts, paedophiles and sociopaths, many fail to real-ise that perhaps the most immediate threat emanates from their children's peers, as increasing numbers of kids use the internet to terrorise and alienate other students at school and at home. This new form of intimidation is proliferating as young people spend more and more time online, more often than not without any adult supervision.

What is cyberbullying?

The term 'cyberbullying' was first used by the creator of the website www.bullying.org, Canadian educator Bill Belsey, to refer to the use of online or mobile technology to harass or intimidate another person. Cyberbullying has become pervasive due to the growth of rapid, potentially anonymous electronic communication, from instant messaging, forums, email and chatrooms to personal and social networking sites, putting wired children everywhere at risk.

The internet promotes long-distance, arms-length, anonymous communications. Users often feel they can say what they like and often pretend to be someone else, adopting a new cyberguise for different chat rooms and blogs, and this can make them willing to do and say things on the net that they would be unlikely to do in person. Psychologists call this 'disinhibition'.

The phenomenon of disinhibition has turned on its head the traditional image of the bully waiting behind the bike shed. They have been replaced by a 24-hour, wireless, anonymous version who instead hides behind text messages, MSN, MySpace and

YouTube. Technology has created and empowered a new breed of bully – children who can comfortably bully from their computer or mobile phone, at a time and place of their choosing.

In contrast to more conventional face-to-face bullying, cyberbullying doesn't allow time for reflection between planning and implementing an intimidating act. The technology creates an illusion of invisibility for the cyberbully – they receive no tangible visual or auditory feedback, dramatically reducing any likelihood of the bully feeling some empathy. They can remain largely unaware of the consequences for their victims. Today's perpetrators, fuelled by an immature brain and little life experience, often believe they have some sort of cloak of immortality. The lightning-fast, faceless nature of the abuse gives perpetrators a false sense of power and invincibility – a sort of digital dutch courage. Many assume – correctly – that their victims won't tell, and as a result they can get away with saying anything online.

The broad reach of cyberspace can deliver the bullying message to a potentially huge audience and, abetted by the use of aliases, can make it difficult to track down the cyberbullies. The ensuing confusion as to their identity may even add to the perpetrator's power trip. Also, unlike the old-fashioned schoolyard bully, the digital version need not be bigger and stronger than the victim. Thanks to the levelling power of technology, the tormentor may be several years younger and physically weaker.

What makes cyberbullying particularly unpleasant is that, in our 'always-on' society, it can happen around the clock. It doesn't end when the child arrives home. In the past, such cruelty was largely confined to trips to and from school, recess and lunchtimes in the schoolyard. Now, victims cannot necessarily escape the harassment by reaching the safety of home.

Online messages range in nastiness from 'You're gay' to 'We know where you live – we're going to burn your house down' or even 'Why don't you kill yourself?' Adding to the misery, the written word appears more concrete. It can be read repeatedly and is often experienced as more 'real' than fleeting spoken abuse. It can be so invasive that a child or teen feels trapped and helpless and in many instances will not report what is going on.

Cyberbullying has grabbed the headlines from time to time,

when tragic events such as the Columbine High School massacre are shown to have involved elements of online threats. It is crucial to understand that all cyberbullying, even less dramatic incidents such as the spreading of rumours and simply saying mean things online, can be very harmful and are deserving of the attention of parents, schools and the authorities. Any cyberbullying can erode a child's self-esteem and confidence and can lead to later academic difficulties, interpersonal problems and psychological distress, including depression and anxiety. These problems can be exacerbated when not taken seriously by adults. The worst response is to trivialise these incidents, instructing victims to 'just ignore it'. Although psychological harm caused by cyberbullying may be less readily apparent than the consequences of a physical bullying encounter, it is no less serious.

Types of cyberbullying

There are many types of digital malice, which seem to mutate over time as the technology evolves. All are designed to scare and belittle via a direct attack or something more devious, such as when a message, photograph or website is spread around like a rumour, damaging an individual's image and inciting gossip or worse. Research commissioned by the Anti-Bullying Alliance from Goldsmiths College, University of London, identifies seven categories of cyberbullying:

- **Text message bullying** involves sending unwelcome texts that are threatening or cause discomfort.

- **Picture/video clip bullying via mobile phone cameras** is used to make the person being bullied feel threatened or embarrassed, with images usually sent to other people. 'Happy slapping' involves filming and sharing images of physical attacks, as with the notorious Werribee DVD (see chapter 4, page 72).

- **Phone call bullying via mobile phone** uses silent calls or abusive messages. Sometimes the bullied person's phone is stolen and used to harass others, who then think the phone owner is responsible. As with all mobile phone bullying, perpetrators often disguise their numbers, sometimes using someone else's phone to avoid being identified.

- **Email bullying** makes use of email to send bullying or threatening messages, often with an invented pseudonym or using someone else's name to pin the blame on them.
- **Chatroom bullying** involves sending menacing or upsetting responses to children or young people when they are in a web-based chatroom.
- **Bullying through Instant Messaging (IM)** is an internet-based form of bullying where children and young people can be sent unpleasant messages as they conduct real-time conversations online.
- **Bullying via websites** includes the use of defamatory web logs (blogs), personal websites and online personal polling sites. Social networking sites for young people also provide opportunities for cyberbullying.

How common is it?

One of the first studies on the prevalence of cyberbullying in Australia was conducted by Marilyn Campbell at the Queensland

University of Technology. She found about 11 per cent of the Year 8 students surveyed said that they partook in cyber-bullying as a bully, while about 14 per cent said they were victims. Twenty-five per cent said that they knew somebody who had been cyberbullied, and over half said they believed that this kind of bullying was on the increase.

Other Australian research projects suggest that online bully-ing is on the increase. A 2006 internet survey I conducted of some 13 000 readers of *Girlfriend* magazine found that 42 per cent had been bullied online. Also, the *Herald Sun* (1 March 2007) reported that a 2006 poll of 650 Melbourne school students, con-ducted by the University of Melbourne's Faculty of Education, found 32 per cent of students aged 12–17 reported being cyber-bullied, and of those victims 30 per cent said it happened several times or more during a single school term.

An interesting facet of this last research was that girls were two and a half times more likely than boys to be victims. Cyber-bullying may be especially attractive to girls, who are usually socialised to abstain from physical aggression towards others.

Girls are more likely to bully each other through 'relational methods'. That is, girls wound each other by spreading rumours and excluding each other from activities. Using the internet to spread gossip and rumours represents an effective new tool in girls' repertoire of bullying behaviours.

What are the signs your child is being cyberbullied?

The signs of a cyberbullied child are not dissimilar to those displayed by any victim of more traditional bullying, including psychosomatic symptoms such as unexplained headaches, stomach upsets, nausea, bed-wetting, insomnia and night terrors.

By picking up the typical signals, parents will be able to provide help and support at an early stage. Early intervention and prompt action can do much to resolve the issue. Australia's NetAlert articulates seven common signs that may indicate to parents that their children are being bullied online:

- spending a lot of time on the computer

- having trouble sleeping or having nightmares
- feeling depressed or crying without reason
- mood swings
- feeling unwell
- becoming anti-social and losing friends
- falling behind in homework.

The non-profit Cyberbullying.org website adds other warning signs, including:

- unexplained long-distance telephone call charges
- not saying who they are talking to
- unexplained pictures on computer
- sudden fear of going out of the house
- frequent complaints of illness before school or community events
- frequent visits to the school nurse or office complaining of feeling sick – wants to call parents to come and get them
- lowered self-esteem
- marked change in attitude, dress or habits

- stories, excuses that don't seem to make sense
- acting out aggression at home
- missing or incomplete schoolwork, decreased success in class.

While such lists are helpful guides, the truth is that the signs your child may be the target of cyberbullying can be incredibly subtle, and many of them are also typical signs of adolescents who are in the process of navigating their developmental cyclone, with hormones running amok and rapid neuronal changes taking place.

The no-brainer signs remain the key behavioural indicators, including school refusal and irregular and secretive internet use. Screens being minimised every time a parent walks past is a signal always worth investigating, as is an unexpected refusal to log on. Another sign is a sudden tendency to avoid answering their mobile phone, or conversely, a constant habit of nervously checking it. In general, look for change in normal behaviour, mood and general demeanour, particularly after internet or mobile phone use.

Combating cyberbullying

A frequent problem for parents in dealing with their child being cyberbullied is the victim's reluctance to admit what's happening. The child may fear that 'dobbing' may encourage worse bullying, or that parents will react by taking away the computer, the mobile phone or their internet access privileges. Your wired child should be assured that it is understood that they haven't done anything wrong to deserve cyberbullying, and that they won't be punished by being cut off from their online lives.

A good piece by Amanda Paulson in *The Christian Science Monitor* (30 December 2003) pointed out that as cyberbullying shares much with its more face-to-face variety, many of the techniques in combating it are the same, namely:

1. Teach young people to report incidents.
2. Don't engage the bully.
3. Talk about the issues surrounding bullying at school and at home.

In addition, parents can do much to prevent the problems from occurring in the first place. Cyberbullying.org has good recommendations for preventative measures, which I've paraphrased here:

- Remember, keeping computers in an open, commonly used space at home helps with supervision. Be aware that wireless networks and laptops can provide 24/7 net access anywhere in and even around the house, but they can be restricted to specific computers or set to require passwords.

- Again, make internet access conditional on following the rule of a complete prohibition on revealing personal information online, including real names and birth date, names of friends or family, identifying pictures, email addresses, postal address, mobile phone number, and school name (or extracurricular team and club names). There should also be an absolute prohibition against revealing passwords or PIN numbers, except to parents or guardians. Agree on a rule where kids must ask permission before sharing any information with anyone, including when registering a product purchased for your computer (like a game).

- Young people should be encouraged to retain a healthy scepticism – remind them they can never be sure someone online is who they say they are.
- Children should be taught 'netiquette' – good manners on the net. They should be encouraged to be polite to others online, just as they would offline, and to not respond to rude or mean people. Just like traditional bullies, they are trying to provoke a reaction, and they shouldn't be given the satisfaction or the power.
- It's wise to learn never to send messages to someone when upset. After the moment has passed, most will regret having sent an angry message, and once sent, it is hard to undo the damage – you can't put toothpaste back in the tube!
- Children should be taught to never open a message from someone they don't know. If they're in doubt, they should ask their parents or guardian.
- Trust your instincts and teach your kids to trust theirs – if it

doesn't look or feel right, it probably isn't. Tell your kids that if they find something while surfing the net that they don't like, makes them feel uncomfortable or scares them, they should close it or shut the computer down and tell you or a supervising adult.

- Young people don't have to be online 24/7. Parents should feel entitled to encourage their sons and daughters to turn off, disconnect and unplug and try some actual reality instead of virtual reality! Negotiate a balance between school work, internet socialising and the all-important time with family and friends offline, which research says can be a major protective factor in their lives.

All families should consider an internet safety plan (see chapter 8). Parents should consult with their offspring and draw up an online contract, which outlines the agreed rules for the family's internet use. It could include safety guidelines, such as some of those described above, which will help protect against cyberbullies.

What should you do if your child is a victim?

The most important thing is to ensure your children know that you understand it isn't their fault if they become a victim of cyberbullying, and that they should come to you and tell you about it. You can counsel them, first, to not reply to cyberbullies' taunts. Your children should realise that responding rewards the bully, and that heated responses can even lead to unwelcome counteraccusations that implicate the original victim in a two-way fight.

It is also unwise for you or your children to try and make contact directly with someone who you suspect might be the cyberbully. This should be handled by the appropriate authorities, such as schools and, in some cases, the police.

Instead, several actions can immediately be taken.

Blocking the bullies

Email applications can be set to block mails from specified senders, which provides at least a quick first step to avoiding contact from a bully. Similarly, instant messaging services enable you to block (or 'ignore' or 'ban') specified contacts, and these should be set immediately to prevent further messages from a bully. Of course, these measures are readily circumvented by a determined bully (who can use different names and identities), and it may prove necessary to delete your child's email and IM accounts and start afresh with new ones. If so, a new opportunity arises to keep addresses and usernames secret from all but the most trusted people.

You might have your child set their mobile phone to use a caller-ID block, which blocks their number from being seen by others. This helps restrict the people who know their number to those who need it – you, other trusted adults and perhaps closest friends.

Informing the authorities

It is important to report instances of cyberbullying to appropriate authorities, who can provide advice or are empowered to act to protect your child.

- Contact your child's school immediately, via email so there is a record of your complaint, and seek an immediate meeting.

- Contact your ISP (Internet Service Provider).
- Ring the NetAlert Helpline: 1800 880 176.
- Report the bullying to police.

Website host companies can remove offensive and defamatory websites. You can often determine the company that hosts an offending site, and find their contact details.

Physical threats especially should be reported to your local police – it is a criminal offence to menace or harass people. State police services have specialist units dealing with electronic crime.

Saving the evidence

While your children should avoid reading bullying messages, it is recommended that they not be deleted. Saved emails, IM chats and the like are evidence which can be useful to ISPs, phone companies and the police. Cyberbullying.info suggests that when saving emails you should ensure the email application has 'Display Full Headers' selected, which displays (and saves) more details about the sender.

Install protective software

Finally, especially if you have young children, you may choose to install software which can help protect them from cyberbullies. Applications such as eMailTrackerPro can trace the origin of suspect emails, and block them, and several applications now exist to monitor IM programs. These monitoring applications, such as ChatAlert! and ChatBlocker, keep watch on IM, chat and website browsing according to parameters chosen by you – they scan for offending language (including that used by potential online predators), and some also block outgoing messages with passwords and credit card details or set time limits for use of specific services. When dangerous language is detected, or other limits are breached, programs can respond by providing the child with onscreen warnings, or even email and SMS you directly. By responding to parental alerts – wherever you are – you are enabled to warn your child, break their communications by closing the application, or even shut down their computer.

Case Study

Katy had just moved to a new school. She was quite shy and felt very fortunate when she was befriended by a very popular girl called Jane. Jane introduced her to others and in a very short time she easily fitted in and became 'one of the girls'. After a year or so Katy and Jane became best friends. They would do virtually everything together, hanging out at school, playing sport together and sharing their secrets. During that first year Katy and Jane exchanged their MSN usernames and passwords. Katy just saw this as something best friends did. But in her second year at school, towards the end of second term, the girls had a huge fight, with Jane accusing Katy of trying to steal her boyfriend. The relationship ended in a flurry of bitterness and recrimination and there was no contact between the girls during the holidays. When she returned to school after the holidays, Katy noticed that virtually no one talked to her. The most upsetting thing was that her normal group of friends, the one she'd usually hang out with at lunch and recess, completely ignored her.

As she walked from class to class, she started to notice other people in the school, even people she did not know very well, gesturing at her and whispering and laughing amongst themselves. The moment school was over she switched on her mobile phone and to her horror discovered around sixty text messages calling her a slut, a whore and a bitch. Katy was mystified. This went on for days but she elected not to tell her parents because she was embarrassed and hoped it would just blow over.

But things began to get even worse. Katy started receiving emails, many from people she didn't know, saying terrible things about what she had allegedly done, hurling insults and questioning her morality and values.

```
Don't come to school again or you'll die.
Move to another school slut!
```

Katy logged on to MSN and found that there was hardly anyone online, but she soon realised that the people she normally communicated with were blocking her. She got a text message telling her to visit a website which she discovered had an image of her face superimposed upon a naked girl engaged in lewd behaviour. The site displayed a range of disparaging statements about her, ranging from mildly offensive through to the pornographic, none of which were true. People were invited to post comments.

This was the final straw for Katy and she decided to tell her parents. They contacted their ISP. The next day someone set up a blog about Katy, with more pictures and a list of new lies and rumours. People from neighbouring schools joined in and also posted comments about her. This went on for several troubling weeks. Her ISP investigated and she was advised to put a spam filter on her account so that only emails from her address book could be received. She also blocked all the people in her contact list who were sending her nasty messages.

Unfortunately this was not enough to deter the perpetrators, and she continued to receive offensive and threatening text messages from people: 'Why don't u just die?' That's when Katy's parents contacted the police, who traced the numbers and visited those responsible. The police discovered that Katy had supposedly sent all her friends a message telling them that she had slept with the entire school football team, and boasting that she had tricked many of the guys into cheating on their girlfriends, many of whom had been Katy's good friends. It finally dawned on Katy that it was her former 'friend' Jane who had initiated much of what had happened. Jane must have logged on to MSN using Katy's username and password and then sent the malicious message to everyone on Katy's contact list.

When Katy's parents confronted Jane, she admitted what she had done but said it was just a joke and she hadn't meant for everyone to take it so seriously. Jane's parents were completely unaware of their daughter's actions. But for Katy it had caused tremendous stress, making school life very difficult and causing her to lose many of her friends.

Katy actually handled this situation well, in that she told her parents what was happening, which led to the school shutting down the message board. She had blocked all the emails from people she didn't know and saved all the abusive and threatening messages that she received on MSN and her mobile, which were used legally as evidence. What she should never have done is to have given her personal details (username and password) to a friend – she never imagined that doing so could affect her whole life. Like many teenagers Katy's age, she couldn't see around corners.

What should you do if your child is a cyberbully?

In a perfect world – with proper education, a well-executed internet safety agreement and adequate monitoring and supervision – all the online behaviour of your wired child would be in accord with your family's values of kindness and respect for others. However, as I often point out, young people have a characteristic inability to predict the consequences of their actions, because their prefrontal cortex (the voice of reason) is often not fully mature until their early twenties.

Impulse control, planning ahead and risk assessment are not always well developed faculties at a young age and, as a result of their immature moral development and underdeveloped sense of empathy, many cyberbullies may rationalise their actions on the basis that everyone else is doing it, that they won't get caught or that their victim deserved it. More often than not, my interviews with cyberbullies reveal they never really thought through the consequences of their behaviour. They say 'It was just a joke'. Schoolchildren often talk about 'pranking' in connection with sending rude, offensive or harassing messages via text. It needs to be clearly understood that pranking is not a legal concept and that the law regards this behaviour as an assault, for which there can be serious penalties.

So what should parents do if they make the devastating

discovery that their offspring has been anonymously sending a stream of vicious messages to ridicule and threaten a schoolmate? Given the seriousness – and potential criminality – associated with cyberbullying, parents should take such a discovery very seriously. If your child is engaging in cyberbullying, you will have the biggest influence in changing his or her behaviour.

The principles involved in responding to a cyberbully are the same as for regular schoolyard bullying, in that once parents are made aware of their child's actions they should seek to get the facts (remember that the child may be responding in kind to bullying they have received, which doesn't reduce their culpability but may be important information for schools or the courts); confront any denial; discuss the child's thoughts and feelings; and ensure that the behaviour stops, and that the cyberbully understands the unacceptability of their actions. If it is a relatively in-house affair, not involving outside agencies (schools or police), then the parents should impose appropriate and immediate consequences and increase vigilance for a while. It is much better if the consequences of such behaviour had been talked through beforehand and therefore come as no surprise.

As to the nature and extent of any consequences, a common parental response may be a period of time offline, along with suspension of other privileges which may be appropriate depending on the severity of their actions. The consequences should be immediate, enforceable (take the modem/router with you to work!), time-limited (don't punish them for months on end or they will forget what they are being punished for and just build up resentment – short and sharp is preferable) and supported by all the adults in the family. Any differences of opinion or deviation in the application of the consequences lessen their impact considerably.

In some instances, the first parents will know of their offspring being a cyberbully will be when the school authorities or police inform them. This may be extremely traumatic for the whole family, as well as the perpetrator. The family's job in such situations is to adopt a position of 'we love you but we don't love your behaviour'. The consequences imposed by both their school and the courts may be severe and the young person will need family support to cope with the process and to be given the opportunity to rebuild the trust that has been lost.

As with any potential problems arising from the online lives of children, the best defence against cyberbullying is a watchful, involved parent, guardian, family member or friend. It's axiomatic in psychology that if you make your values, rules and expectations clear to children from an early age, and follow this up with warnings and consistent consequences (à la Jo Frost, TV's *Supernanny*), then most young people will respond positively. Your adolescent should feel safe, valued and listened to, in a child–parent relationship based on trust and mutual respect. You can buy the latest turbo-charged internet filters, monitoring software and a variety of gizmos, but the trouble is, the methods available to cyberbullies are as broad as the technology and their imaginations allow, and young people are ingenious in their capacity to get around the defences you put in place. Many adults call on ISPs and schools to take more responsibility also, and there are signs that they are making serious efforts to tackle the problems. But a well-balanced, trusted child in a communicative family with sensible rules in place is best placed to deal with whatever kinds of bullying the world presents.

There certainly seems to be a consensus backed by research across the western world that cyberbullying is real, on the increase and capable of great harm. If we are not to fulfill the prophecy of some doomsayers who paint a picture of a *Lord of the Flies* cyber-realm, where our children are at the mercy of digital thugs un-policed by parents, then it is time that parents stepped up to the plate.

Chapter 6

Is there such a thing
as internet addiction?

In 2005, a young man died from presumed heart failure after a marathon online game session in South Korea, one of the world's most wired nations. Eating and sleeping very little, he reportedly played the game StarCraft at an internet café for fifty hours with few breaks before collapsing. Apparently, nine other South Koreans died in 2005 after similar binges. Chinese state media also more recently reported the death of an obese man after he spent nearly his entire seven-day holiday break playing online games.

Can we dismiss these cases as bizarre aberrations or are they a tragic glimpse of a possible fate for those of our children who spend too much of their time online? Is there such a thing as internet addiction? If there is, how would you know if your child is a sufferer? The scientific jury is still out.

Debate about internet addiction started in 1995 when Dr Ivan Goldberg dreamt up the concept of Internet Addiction Disorder (IAD), drawing strong parallels with pathological gambling as diagnosed by the DSM-IV TR – the mental health 'bible' used by psychiatrists and psychologists to categorise mental illnesses. Some mental health professionals want IAD officially recognised in future as a unique disorder, while others argue it is byproduct of existing disorders.

For the moment at least, IAD is a 'Clayton's' diagnosis – the diagnosis you are having when you are not having a diagnosis. In other words, technically, no such disorder exists.

Nonetheless, in 1995 US psychologist Kimberly Young established a Centre for Online Addiction to treat those deemed internet addicts, and similar clinics have been established in China, South Korea and Sweden. A game addiction clinic opened in Amsterdam in 2006, claiming about 20 per cent of all gamers develop a dependency on gaming.

Clinical addiction or not, there is plenty of evidence that some people use the internet so much that it causes problems in their lives, and there is also reason to believe that overuse is becoming prevalent.

How widespread is the problem? According to a 2006 survey conducted by Stanford University's Impulse Control Disorders Clinic, 'more than one out of eight Americans exhibited at least one possible sign of problematic internet use'. Compulsive use went beyond the stereotype of pornography and gambling, to include chatrooms, shopping sites, special-interest sites and email. The researchers found that 12.4 per cent stayed online longer than intended very often or often and 5.9 per cent felt their relationships suffered as a result of excessive internet use. The head of the study, Elias Aboujaoude, said he found most concerning the numbers of people who hid their non-essential internet use from others (8.7 per cent) or used the internet to escape problems or relieve a negative mood (8.2 per cent), much in the same way that alcoholics might.

As far as teenagers are concerned, the most recent research in Australia was conducted by Dr Rahamatulla Mubarak Ali of Flinders University, who surveyed private and state secondary school students. He found that 'just over a quarter of the students surveyed said they used the internet on a daily basis and considered it to be an important part of their lives; seven per cent said they were becoming addicted to the routine of accessing the internet'. On average, the teenagers spent thirteen hours a week online.

Heavy internet use doesn't leave discarded syringes on the street or cause obvious damage to persons or property, so it can be less apparent than alcohol or substance abuse. Also, as a social, interactive medium loaded with information, it seems a world away from something like gambling abuse, a solitary activity with no redeeming social value. Is compulsive internet use alarming, then?

Problems seem to arise when young people use the internet as a substitute for human interaction, which may interfere with the successful completion of developmental tasks (see my book *Surviving Adolescents* for more on development). They find themselves depressed, anxious and socially isolated. Flinders University's Dr Mubarak said that a trend in recent American research shows that 'chatroom use tends to reduce interactions between adolescents and their families, producing negative effects on family cohesiveness and increasing the potential for isolation and psychological problems including depression'.

Online gaming features prominently in stories of problematic internet use, especially in light of its connection to the tragic deaths I've mentioned. Much of the focus is on the Massively Multiplayer Online Role-Playing Games (MMORPGs), in which a large number of players interact with one another in a virtual world. In an interview with online magazine *TwitchGuru*, clinical psychologist Dr Maressa Orzack, founder of Computer Addiction Services in Massachusetts, estimated that as many as 40 per cent of players of the popular MMORPG *World of Warcraft* players are addicted. She said the unending scenarios of MMORPGs are designed to keep people in the game, making them inherently addictive.

As well as the problems caused by games designed to be never-ending quests, there are other possible psychological factors at play, such as the drive to not give up an activity to which much time has already been committed, lest it seem to have been time wasted (a compulsion known as 'sunk cost fallacy'). It's also thought possible that gaming produces the chemical dopamine, which stimulates the brain's pleasure system. This might lead to an ever-increasing desire to play the game and a 'downer' in between sessions. It all makes for a potent brew.

Switching off for sleep

NetAlert's 2005 study with ninemsn, mentioned in chapter 2, revealed a huge gap between parents' and their children's under-standing of family rules for time spent online. While 80 per cent of parents claimed to have set ground rules for net use, only 69 per cent of the teenagers agreed that such rules existed.

It is also very common for parents to hear the chirping of mobile phones from their kids' rooms all night. A mother recently told me that she confiscated her daughter's phone then put it by her own bed and went to sleep. She found she was woken from its beeping all night. There is an interesting parallel here in nature – it is thought the dawn chorus is produced by birds checking to see who survived the night. I wonder whether the mobiles chirping all night perform a similar function.

Some years ago clinical psychologist Andrew Fuller revealed that 90 per cent of Year 10 students were sleep-deprived because they were staying up late on the net or using their mobile phones all night to communicate with one another, or both.

Many parents are unaware that widespread research indicates that adolescents require nine and a quarter hours of sleep each night. Young people also naturally want to have their block of sleep later than adults. Research led by Professor Till Roenneberg at the Ludwig-Maximilians-Universität, Munich, suggests that as children mature, they naturally go to bed and get up later. He told Britain's *Telegraph* (13 January 2007) that 'teens want to go to bed two hours later than 40 to 50-year-olds, and in 10 per cent there is a four hour delay.'

So if your early teen goes to bed at 11 p.m. and gets to sleep at midnight, in order for them to get an adequate amount of sleep they would have to get up at 9.15 a.m. Of course, you're waking them up at 7 a.m. to get ready for school, so if that pattern repeats five nights a week, they will rapidly build up a sleep debt of ten hours.

Given that plenty of research shows that lack of sleep can affect academic performance and can seriously compromise learning – as well as being strongly linked to increases in anxiety, depression, poor immunity, accidents, poor judgement, memory and slower reactions – this should be of concern to all parents. It might also prompt the incorporation of rules about allowable time on the net into a family internet safety contract (see chapter 8).

Case Study

Henry presented in my office with his mother, who explained to me that she was concerned about her son's internet use. In Year 8, at the age of 13, he was introduced to an online computer game called *RuneScape* and now some eight years later he can play this fantasy MMORPG for up to fifteen hours a day. Henry has few friends other than those he speaks to via his headset as he plays.

The game is set in a fictional Tolkienesque world called Gielinor. With over nine million active players *RuneScape* is among the most popular online games in the world. From 3 p.m., when Henry usually wakes up, he logs on and embarks on a virtual journey fighting monsters, gathering treasure and embarking on quests across the various kingdoms of Gielinor. He can play for twelve to fifteen hours a day, stopping only to eat and sleep. The game has become his life.

Since every player's character has a set of skills that can be improved, the more Henry practises, the higher his character's skill rating. A higher skill level unlocks new items and abilities that further add to a character's power. Henry has been playing for so long that he belongs to the top clan and enjoys a high overall rating, which is visible to other players and shows his experience. He is ranked among the top 1000 players in the world.

The problem for Henry is that although he is very bright, he has tackled virtually none of the developmental tasks required for a 20-year-old, he has few friends, goes out very rarely, experiences anxiety and depressive symptoms when not playing, and is completely reliant on his parents for everything. There is increasing discord at home as his parents attempt to ween him from the game, urging him to go to university, but his sleep patterns and compulsive computer gaming make this very difficult.

With the aid of the parental control program ENUFF PC, which limits the time Henry can spend online, his daily game time has been reduced to nine hours, and he is being forced to consider other ways of using his time. The stranglehold the game has on Henry's life is slowly being loosened.

So, how much is too much?

When all is said and done, how would you know if your child is in danger of suffering from problematic internet behaviour? In order for young people to tackle the developmental tasks of adolescence they need a balanced lifestyle, a variety of interests and clear rules and guidelines that can be relaxed as they grow up. If a young person spends so much time on the net that other parts of their lives are neglected, we clearly have a problem.

Australia's advisory body NetAlert cautions parents to look for children who are:

- Always talking about a particular online activity such as a game or website.
- Breaking the rules of the family internet safety contract (see chapter 8) in relation to time spent online or download limits.
- Preferring to spend more time online than with other family members or friends.
- Acting aggressively or violently towards others.

- Feeling tired in the day from being up late at night or generally complaining about poor health.
- Falling behind in school work with more time being spent on non-essential internet use than on homework.
- Always wanting newer and faster computers and access to the internet.

US psychologist Dr Kimberly Young, author of *Caught in the Net*, has also developed a quick test for parents to determine whether their child might have an internet 'addiction'. It is accessible on the website of the Center for Internet Addiction Recovery, of which Dr Young is director, at www.netaddiction.com/resources/parents_test.htm.

What can you do to guard against addictive use?

The boffins can't seem to reach agreement on when a tickle becomes a passion, a passion a compulsion and a compulsion a habit, or whether internet addiction is a real mental illness.

Having said that, there is a growing consensus among psychologists that there is a problem with a number of young people using the internet in a compulsive manner, in a way not seen before with other forms of communications or technology.

The final word goes to US psychologist Dr David Greenfield, author of *Virtual Addiction*: 'If you speak with any group of mental health professionals, half to three quarters will say that they have seen in their practice people who have issues with this. All addictions are really about numbing out pain and that pattern of numbing and pleasure-seeking becomes habitual. Most probably because of elevated levels of dopamine, which is consistent across many behavioural and substance based addictions.'

The reluctance to take this seriously as a clinical issue in part stems from the proliferation of 'addictions' identified in the popular media, such as in April Lane Benson's *I Shop Therefore I Am: Compulsive Buying & the Search for Self*, Patrick Carnes' *Out of the Shadows: Understanding Sexual Addiction*, Kay Sheppard's *From the First Bite: A Complete Guide to Recovery from Food*

Addiction and even Joyce Meyer's *Approval Addiction: Overcoming Your Need to Please Everyone*, 2005.

Whether internet addiction is officially recognised or not, parents should use commonsense. Not overusing the net should be part of your children's education from their earliest online experiences. Revisit the basic principles of keeping your children safe in Cyberia listed in 'Bringing the digital family together', on page 23.

If your offspring gets to the point where compulsive internet use is negatively interfering with their normal developmental tasks (such as making friends and doing school work) or their health, and they are starting to neglect peers, parents and siblings and putting a strain on relationships – in the first instance, you shouldn't panic. Instead, choose an appropriate time, sit down and discuss your concerns with them. Agree on a family internet safety contract (see chapter 8) which sets clearly understood rules, such as the time of day they're allowed online, the length of time allowed in a session, and so on. It should involve parental monitoring and a modification of the original, worrying behaviour. Talking with your child's teachers and other parents will assist in obtaining an overall view of your children's internet usage compared with others in their peer group.

If a problem is emerging, and agreed time limits are being regularly ignored, you might consider parental control software that allows you to set automated limits.

Failing this, you should seek professional help from a psychologist who can help children identity problem behaviours and learn coping skills to regulate their use. Be warned: not all psychologists have an interest in adolescents or problematic internet use. To find the nearest qualified psychologist with such a specialisation, contact the Australian Psychological Society Referral Service on 1800 333 497 (toll free).

TANDBERG

Chapter 7
Schools and cybersafety

Schools need to help young people develop a moral compass as they stroll through the back alleys of Cyberia. While students know the online language and the rituals, the reality is that few adults at home have ever had a conversation with them about what is socially acceptable and what is not in this brave new world. The digital generation gap has become a chasm in this respect because while most adults (including those in schools) can relate to schoolyard bullying, they have no context for understanding how the behaviour manifests itself in the virtual world. Similarly, they sometimes find it hard to conceive of the various ways unfettered online access can provide a gateway to unsafe and unwanted behaviour.

Newspapers are increasingly filled with stories of internet-related problems at schools. A small sample reveals the extent of the issues. *The Daily Telegraph* (22 August 2006) reported that

Sydney's Castle Hill Public School suspended an 11-year-old boy for showing pornographic images around school which he'd downloaded on to his mobile phone. The following month *The Sunday Telegraph* (3 September 2006) reported that five boys were suspended or expelled from Sydney's exclusive King's School during August for cyberbullying. The Principal, Dr Timothy Hawkes, said, 'The school has taken a hard line . . . because bullying at schools can spread like cancer'. In their investigation into cyberbullying in schools, *The Advertiser* (4 December 2006) reported that South Australian Electronic Crimes Unit Detective Senior Sergeant Barry Blundell said 'children were being cautioned, sent to family conferences or put before the courts because of criminal behaviour online'. The Victorian Government's plan to ban state school access to video website YouTube was reported in *The Age* (1 March 2007), with the Education Minister saying that school computers should be restricted to 'age-appropriate material relevant to the curriculum and their learning needs'.

These news stories show how much technological developments have changed both the primary and secondary school environments. Today's students commonly have mobile phones – McNair Ingenuity Research's 'Australian Kids Consumer Insights' (April 2003) reported that a quarter of children aged 6–13 have a mobile phone, and over a third aged 10–13. The Department of Communications, Information Technology and the Arts says 82 per cent of Australians 14 years and over used a mobile phone in June 2006. Most phones are now internet-enabled. Many primary and secondary schools also require that students own a laptop, or lend them one, and this is no longer restricted to the wealthier private school system.

The legal obligation of every school to provide a safe environment for young people to learn now extends to doing everything possible to prevent students accessing offensive or inappropriate material, or using their online access in a harmful way. As the internet has become a centrepiece of the educational system, all schools should have an online safety policy that protects their students, perhaps tailored to different age levels. This chapter outlines what we should expect from schools and how to approach them with concerns.

What should parents expect from schools?

The key to a successful school online safety program is dissemination. An 'acceptable use agreement' should be distributed to staff, students and parents, irrespective of whether they make use of the school's computer network and internet facilities. It should clearly outline the obligations, responsibilities and range of consequences connected with any breaches of the agreement. Copies should be signed, by parents for younger primary schoolchildren and by the children themselves at higher school levels, and kept by the school and at home.

A good acceptable use agreement (see below for links to examples) will include guidelines similar to those I've recommended for parents to apply at home. It will advise safe net practices, such as keeping passwords private and not revealing personal details or sending personal images. It will direct students to report inappropriate material or behaviour, and explicitly ban personal attacks online, including anything discriminatory, prejudiced or defamatory. There will likely be restrictions governing subscription to discussion groups and, of course, a ban on illegal activities.

Most schools will require that their computing and net facilities are limited to educational purposes. They may reserve the right to monitor their facilities' use, including personal email traffic and browsing on their network, even outside school hours, and downloaded and saved files.

Of course, students very often bring their own internet-enabled devices (laptops, mobile phones and handheld PDAs) to school. The issue of whether students should be allowed to bring phones with cameras to school was first raised in 2003 by the West Australian state opposition, who argued that the government should restrict their use in schools due to the threat to students' privacy. To deal with internet-enabled phones, some schools have asked students to drop theirs in a secure box before classes start, or face having them confiscated.

Schools will differ on what personal net-enabled items they allow students to bring on-site, but they should make their students clearly aware of their policies. For example, a school may claim the right to inspect a student's private mobile phone if there is a suspicion of a breach of their use agreement. If suspicions are serious enough, refusal could potentially lead to police warrants.

It is also expected that schools will install filtering software to restrict access to certain websites and services, from pornography to social networking. The degree to which internet access is restricted will differ from institution to institution – you might ask what censoring takes place at your child's school.

As discussed in chapter 4, page 83, the Victorian Government has banned access to the video-sharing site YouTube in state schools, in a bid to tackle the growing problem of cyberbullying. Cyberbullying is a major problem and student welfare teachers report that they daily deal with the psychological fallout from an abusive email sent overnight or exclusion from instant messages on the weekend, and the subsequent deterioration in social relationships that follow. This has an impact on the whole school community. But while schools should have filters and blocks in place, they cannot be relied upon to eradicate problems associated with certain websites. It is relatively easy to circumvent filtering software, and it is likely students will already have found ways to get around the block on

YouTube. School bans also don't address the fact that most cyberbullying occurs outside of school hours, in homes or wherever else young people gather and have access to the net (which is now virtually anywhere).

What happens when the rules are broken?

Breaking the rules of a signed use agreement will be taken seriously, especially as it may even involve criminal behaviour. Generally, parents should expect notification from the school if it is suspected that their child has breached the agreement, or been a victim of a breach.

The school should have clear guidelines as to the possible penalties for breaking the agreement, which will likely range from the loss of school computer and internet privileges, or payment for any repairs or costs incurred, through to disciplinary action such as suspension and expulsion. The school may deem it necessary to submit details to the police, if the material or behaviour involved constitutes criminal misconduct. It is hoped that any disciplinary action also contain elements that assist the offending student to learn appropriate online behaviour. There should also be scope for parents who disagree with a school's disciplinary action to have their complaints considered.

School cybersafety agreement

While every school is encouraged to draft their own policy in consultation with students, staff, parents and the wider community, most policies will have a similar structure and similar content. NetSafe, the website of the Internet Safety Group of New Zealand, provides a very useful model on their website at www.netsafe.org.nz.

In addition, Victoria's Department of Employment, Education and Training publishes *Safetynet: Internet Usage – Guidelines for Schools* at www.sofweb.vic.edu.au/internet/safety.htm. It includes a list of existing acceptable use policies as samples, which may assist parents to understand the principles and to know what to look for from their child's school:

- **Croydon Secondary College**: www.croydonsc.vic.edu.au/home/policy/
- **PLC Melbourne**: www.plc.vic.edu.au/Library/lis/aup.htm
- **Brentwood Secondary College**: www.brentwood.vic.edu.au/aup1.htm
- **McKinnon Secondary College**: www.mckinnonsc.vic.edu.au/school/aup/aup.htm
- **Kangaroo Flat Primary School**: www.kangarooflatps.vic.edu.au/lrc/page6.html
- **Bendigo Senior Secondary College**: www.bssc.edu.au/administration/policies/online_access/
- **Frankston High School**: www.fhs.vic.edu.au/parents/internet.htm
- **Pakenham Secondary College**: www.pakenhamsc.vic.edu.au/aup.htm
- **Cheltenham Primary School**: www.cheltenhamps.vic.edu.au/parents/internet.html
- **Bayswater Primary School**: www.bayswaterps.vic.edu.au/students/internet.htm

What parents should be doing

In an era when most kids know more about the technology than adults, and are spending up to 1400 hours a year at school, schools need clear policies and guidelines governing the use of their computing and internet facilities, and of personal digital devices brought on-site by students. If you feel your child's school has not addressed the issue, or has not been as proactive as you would like, my strong recommendation is that you advocate on your child's behalf by writing a letter (or email) to the principal, with a copy to the school council or parents and friends organisation. You could include a link to one of the sample use agreements listed in this chapter. You should also request a formal meeting and ask for a response to your concerns.

The impact of any policy is only as good as its implementation, so you might like to ask the school authorities some of these questions about what is being done to protect students.

- How widely has the cybersafety policy been disseminated and understood?
- How does the school curriculum reinforce the policy?

- Has the school provided specific information sessions for parents?
- What mechanisms exist to ensure that reported incidents of cyberbullying, or other inappropriate net use, are never ignored and are handled appropriately?
- Have all school staff received in-service training about the policy?
- Were staff closely involved in the development of the policy?
- Have any staff been specifically trained in handling cyberbullying incidents?
- Is there effective and committed leadership in directing and monitoring the program?

Most schools are well aware of the need to address the issues, especially in the light of the proliferation of media reports, however many are under-resourced and faced with a crowded curriculum. Internet safety policies can be lost in an educational shuffle – a little polite prompting by a group of concerned parents may help.

QUANTITY TIME

QUALITY TIME

Chapter 8

The family internet safety contract

It should be obvious that unlike vinyl records, Super 8 film and floppy disks, the internet is not a passing fad. More than three decades have whizzed by since the birth of the net, and more and more aspects of our lives are going online.

While there is a place for increasing public awareness of online dangers, providing families with internet filters and enacting harsher sentences for internet sexual predators, there is no substitute for parental education. A key recommendation I share with almost all the internet safety authorities across the world is that from the moment children pick up a mouse, the internet 'cyber training wheels' must be introduced then gradually removed as the child develops and demonstrates increasing levels of responsibility.

One of the best ways to do this is to formalise the family's net use. Let's consider how best to go about this, by returning to the household of Chloe, John, Amy and their parents.

If parents want their child to behave responsibly online, they have to set the standards for what they expect. Too often, parents focus only on undesirable behaviours and their parenting styles dissolve into complaining and reacting. If they focus on developing the positive behaviours in their children then the negative behaviours won't be so overwhelming.

Mum and Dad have decided to introduce a family internet safety contract, containing a set of clear and explicit rules about what is and what is not okay when the kids are on the net. It is extremely important for them to make explicit exactly what their expectations of Chloe, John and Amy are as far as their online behaviour is concerned, along with clear, concise consequences if they choose to ignore them. As well as the policies directed at everyone's use, they've decided for now to have a separate section tailored specifically to 8-year-old Amy which includes closer monitoring and restrictions than they feel is necessary for Chloe (14) and John (17).

Initially Chloe was sceptical about the introduction of a

behavioural contract, seeing it as boringly legalistic and probably designed to stop her doing some of the online things she loves. She resisted the idea. Her parents stressed that the contract provided Chloe and the rest of the family with a good record of what had been agreed to, without which internet safety discussions might be forgotten, especially when Chloe might find it convenient to do so. But it also gives her iron-clad guarantees about what her parents have agreed to, including ways she might have the reins loosened in future.

Drawing up a contract is also a positive problem-solving communication for the family. It is an active multi-party negotiation in which Chloe and her siblings have a vested interest. Everyone will want to have their say about conditions of net use, rewards and failures for online behaviour, and the timeframe of the contract and how it can be updated. Chloe's parents will ensure that the clear safety guidelines they have learnt in this book will be its foundation principles. Everything in the contract must be expressed so that any family member old enough to read can understand it.

A good family internet safety contract is designed to obtain and retain compliance. Mum and Dad will have to determine the correct 'currency', or reward. The best contracts provide opportunities for the kids to get as much of what they want by exhibiting appropriate behaviour. Currency is anything that rewards the desired behaviour in order to increase the likelihood of that behaviour occurring again. So what currencies are available to Chloe's parents, in return for safe online practices? These will vary according to age, but for Chloe it might typically involve DVDs, cable television, mobile phones, extra computer privileges and being allowed out with her friends. When Chloe's parents understand what is valuable in her life, they can engage in some shaping of her behaviour.

Once completed, the family internet safety contract should be signed by the whole family, then laminated, blocked or framed and placed near the family computer. The idea is that Chloe and her siblings have discussed its contents and see it in writing, so it's more difficult for them to say they didn't know the rules or didn't understand them. Written agreements provide the children with early lessons in the concept of what it means to sign a binding contract and agree to its stipulations.

With such a contract, Chloe and her siblings are provided with a sense of justice and control, and increased involvement in what goes on in the family. Their direct involvement also increases the likelihood that this is a contract that will 'live and breathe', rather than just being a scrappy piece of paper stuck to the fridge door. Chloe and her siblings now have a document which is the 'final authority', with the signed commitment of all parties to stick to what's been agreed.

Key areas to consider

Every family's different, so every family's contract will be different. You should tailor it to be as specific as you think best, emphasising areas of your greatest concern or addressing particular problem behaviours of your children. You might include specified time limits for net connection, or that mobile phones are switched off after 9 p.m. You might keep it to a simple promise to communicate openly about what's going on in your wired child's online life. But here are some of the key areas you should consider when framing the document, with suggestions for rules.

Don't demonise the net

Include an opening statement acknowledging that the internet is not all evil or stupid and has many wonderful advantages.

Identifying information

Include a clear statement about not providing anyone online with identifying information, including name, address, telephone number, password, parents' names, the name of any club or team they are involved in, or the name of family members' schools. This rule applies for every online activity, including chatrooms, instant messaging, email, personal websites, gaming and social networking. Entering contests and registering for any clubs or other memberships should require parental consent.

Online forms

There should be clear rules against completing questionnaires or any forms online without parents' permission.

Prohibition on revealing details of real life activities

There should also be a total prohibition on family members telling anyone online where they will be or what they will be doing, without parents' permission.

Chatrooms

Children will not enter a chatroom without parents' permission.

Meeting people in real life

Children will not meet in person anyone that they've only met online – unless parents choose to agree and accompany them to meet in a public place.

Restrictions on IM, social networking sites, etc.

Children will only use instant messaging or social networking services with people on their contact/buddy list whom their parents have approved.

Prohibition on cyberbullying

Family members will treat others online as they would have them treat themselves. They will never send out mean or threatening messages nor will they respond to any such messages that are sent to them. Children will report cyberbullying to parents.

Emails

Family members will not open or accept emails, links, URLs or other contacts and information from people they do not know.

Obligation to report distressing material

Children will report to their parents any email, chatroom conversations, instant messages or websites that make them feel uncomfortable, like X-rated images or text. It is understood that it is not their fault if they inadvertently see something bad. If they do see something inappropriate, they will log off or turn off their computer, and tell their parents what happened as soon as possible.

Time restrictions

Children will not go online for longer than the agreed time limits, as negotiated with parents.

Exhibit fiscal responsibility

Children will never go into a new online area that is going to cost additional money without first getting their parents' permission. They will never buy or order products online, or give out any credit card information, without parents' permission.

Awareness of predators and their tricks

Children understand that some predatory people try to befriend kids online, especially targeting those who admit they aren't getting along with their parents or are having a hard time in other areas of their lives.

Public versus private information

Children understand that private family matters should not be discussed online. Instead, they should talk about them with a trusted adult.

Acceptance of parents' right to supervise

Children understand that their parents may supervise their time online and may use a filtering service. This is because they love them and want to ensure their safety.

Online behaviour away from home

Children will not go online at a friend's house, or from a mobile phone, without their parents' permission. They understand that internet use is a privilege, not a right. They will follow their family's internet safety contract at home as well as when they are online elsewhere.

Signature

It is essential that both the child's and parents' signatures are included, with a date from which the contract applies and a date for when the contract can be renegotiated.

A sample contract

ICRA, part of the independent, international organisation Family Online Safety Institute, has developed a Family Online Internet Safety Contract with reference to other online safety pledges and contracts from entities, such as SafeKids.com and i-SAFE America. It is available at www.icra.org/kids/familycontract, and is included on the following pages with their permission as an example of what a contract might look like.

The Family Online Internet Safety Contract

An agreement between

_____ and _____

Child   Parent

Parent Contract

I know that the internet can be a wonderful place for my kids to visit.

I also know that I must do my part to help keep them safe on their visits.

Understanding that my kids can help me, I agree to follow these rules:

1. I will get to know the services and websites my child uses.

2. I will set reasonable rules and guidelines for computer use by my children and I will discuss these rules and post them near the computer as a reminder.

3. I will not overreact If my child tells me about something 'bad' he or she finds or does on the internet.

4. I will try to get to know my child's 'online friends' and 'buddy list' contacts just as I try to get to know his or her other friends.

5. I will try to put the home computer in a family area.

6. I will report suspicious and illegal activity and sites to the proper authorities.

7. I will make or find a list of recommended sites for children.

8. I will frequently check to see where my kids have visited on the internet.

9. I will seek options for filtering and blocking inappropriate internet material from my children.

10. I will talk to my kids about their online explorations and take online adventures with them as often as I can.

I agree to the above.

_____ Date _____

Parent's signature

I understand that my parents have agreed to live by these rules and I agree to help my parents explore the internet with me.

_____ Date _____

Child's signature

Child's Contract

1.   I know that the internet can be a wonderful place to visit. I also know that it is important for me to follow rules that will keep me safe on my visits. I agree to the following rules:

2.   I will choose a safe and sensible screen name for myself that will not reveal personal information about my family or me.

3.   I will keep my password private, except from my parents. I will not sign up for other email accounts without my parents' approval.

4.   I will not put my personal information in my profile. I will not share my personal information, or that of my parents or any other family member, in any way, shape or form, online or with someone I meet online. This includes, but is not limited to, name, address, telephone number, age or school name.

5.   I will treat others the way I want to be treated.

6.   I will use good manners when I'm online, including good language and respect. I will not pick fights or use threatening or mean words.

7.   I will make my own personal safety my priority, since I know there are some people who might be online and pretend to be someone they're not.

8. I will be honest with my parents about people I meet online and will tell them, without always being asked, about these people. I won't answer any emails or instant messages from anyone my parents have not approved.

9. If I see or read things that are bad, icky or mean, I will log off and tell my parents so they can make sure it never happens again.

10. I will tell my parents if I receive pictures, links to bad sites, email or instant messages with bad language or if I'm in a chatroom where people are using swear words or mean and hateful language.

11. I will not send anything to anyone I've met online, without my parents' permission. If I get something from someone I've met online, I'll tell my parents immediately (because that means they have my private information).

12. I will not do anything that someone I've met online asks me to, especially when I know it's something my parents would not be happy about or approve of.

13. I will not call, write a snail mail or meet in person anyone who I've met online without my parents' approval or without a parent coming with me.

14. I understand my parents will supervise my time online and use software to monitor or limit where I go online. They're doing this because they love me and want to protect me.

15. I will teach my parents more about the internet so we can have fun together and learn cool new things.

I agree to the above.

_____ Date _____

Child's signature

I promise to protect my child's safety online by making sure these rules are followed. If my child encounters unsafe situations and tells me, I will handle each situation with maturity and good sense, without blaming anyone, and will calmly work through it with my child to ensure safer internet experiences in the future.

_____ Date _____

Parent's signature

Chapter 9

What to say to your kids

Imagine that Chloe is your daughter, and she has just walked into your bedroom and found you reading this book.

As a digital native with a real wired attitude, she'll probably do an eye roll, maybe even give you a verbal blast, and walk away shaking her head in disgust. On the way to school tomorrow morning, what can you say to her about the fact that you bought the book?

There is a lot you don't know

Explain to the fruit of your loins that you are aware that things have moved along a smidge since the web was first invented and that you know the net is not just a tool for downloading information. You felt that it was important to find out just exactly what young people do online today. The book has made you more curious and you'd really like her to educate you. You no longer want to be a cyber-fossil!

You're being responsible

You should point out that it is your responsibility as a parent to be cautious where there are dangers to your family. You needed to learn more about the dangers and about ways of guarding against them. Remind Chloe that online she is participating in an adult world, where no one's true age or identity can be known. Finding out more about the net is helping you to help her keep safe.

You know the net is not all evil

Tell her that while the book does contain some scary stories, about problematic internet use, cyberbullying and safety breaches, it has also helped you understand that young people are doing wonderfully creative things with the net, and that it has become one of the most highly accessible vehicles for self-expression. You've learnt that young people write, edit and upload their own songs, videos and diary entries for the world to critique and pass around in a way that your generation would never have dreamt of.

You know the net is about communicating with friends and socialising

Tell Chloe that you now understand that the net is an essential part of her social networking and that this is a foreign concept to your generation, which relied on telephones, meetings at coffee shops and dinner parties. Tell her you can see what a great tool this is for staying in touch and up-to-date with old friends and maintaining large circles of friends from wherever you are, which contrasts with your adolescence, when many friends who went overseas just drifted out of your life forever. Explain that while Chloe's online social life might be okay, you've learnt that for others it can sometimes include harassment, the passing around of explicit or doctored photos to show off or get reactions, the use of simple things like party photos taken on camera phones to bully others, nasty gossip via instant messaging, dissing teachers and threatening schools, etcetera. You know that she needs to take care and you want to know if anything bad is happening so you can help. Emphasise that you won't take her offline if she is honest with you.

Everyone is being watched

You've become better aware that what can seem private is rarely so, and you want Chloe to understand that every time she goes online she is being watched. Remind her that in almost every instance peers, parents, police, predators – the entire web public – can see what she's uploading. Net activity leaves digital fingerprints. To help guide the family's safe online life, you will be introducing a family internet safety contract (see chapter 8).

There are serious penalties for net abuse

You have become more aware of some of the legal ramifications of online activities. Since Chloe is over the age of ten, she needs to understand that the police and the courts will hold her responsible for what she does and says online, and you need to be able to help guide her. In addition to the laws of defamation there are a number of state and federal laws governing what is and what is not okay on the net. She needs to understand that you are now up to speed on this part of their lives.

As with all adolescent/parent communication the idea is not to engage in character assassination – or act as if every time they log on they will be hacking into the Pentagon's computers. Remember that overreactions can trigger defensiveness, which shuts down communication.

With young people like Chloe – born into a decade of excess and an interconnected world, the offspring of *The Simpsons* and

The OC, graduates of crèches, products of working families and students of postmodern theory – one must tread carefully. Chloe has no way of understanding how alien this new virtual world of theirs really is to us. Can we really expect her to understand the trepidation we felt when we left the maternity hospital, all those years ago, wondering how we were going to carry such a precious bundle through life? Can we really expect her to understand how life was before car capsules, air bags, mobile phones, DVDs, PDAs, plasma screens or the internet?

To your wired child

If your child cares to accept some words of wisdom from me, it would go like this. Listen to what your parents say about what they've gained from this book. Know that honest and open communication with people who care about you is one of the most significant protective factors you have in the very public space of the net, where peers and malicious strangers can and will do anything they want with the material you upload. The other protective factor – and, truth be known, the best security of all – is your own commonsense. Until you've been around a bit longer, and learnt how to do your own damage control, the fact is that you may need your folks as backup.

But to soothe their anxieties in the meantime there are some really helpful things you could do:

- **Follow the basic safety principles.** Make it a rule that you don't post any information that identifies you personally or gives away your physical location either at home or school, and keep passwords and account details secret, except from your parents. Be healthily suspicious of people's motives online and don't interact with strangers unless you're sure they're not going to end up harassing you – and block them if they do. Don't ever meet anyone in real life without at least one friend with you – better yet, more than one. Ideally, don't do it without telling your parents.

- **Educate your parents.** An educated parent is a more chilled parent. Because they're naturally worried about you and have a legal duty of care, you need a plan to help them. Explain about social networking, etcetera, and show them around a bit. Be their guide and put their minds at rest.

- **Trust your parents.** Talk to them about what you do and don't get alarmed and secretive if they ask you what you've been doing online today. When they know you're doing the right thing, and you're open about it, they'll worry less.

- **Ease their fears.** Your Mum or Dad may read you passages from this book, or show you articles, about truly terrifying things that have actually happened in social networking sites, in online games, etcetera. Many don't get it that these cases aren't the norm, even though I've tried to explain that. So part of your plan should be to help them get some perspective by showing them what your do. With this approach, your parents can be part of the solution rather than part of the problem.

Resources

The following websites are well worth visiting, and were active at the time of writing. I've derived most of their descriptions from the sites themselves.

Australian Communications and Media Authority

www.acma.gov.au

You can report potentially illegal material on websites, forums or in downloaded files to the Australian Communications and Media Authority. The ACMA has online forms for complaints and it is empowered to direct website hosts to remove prohibited content from their service, advise international authorities to do so, or refer cases to appropriate law enforcement agencies. The ACMA also developed the Cybersmart Kids Online site, page 177.

Bullying.org

www.bullying.org

The site of Canadian educator Bill Belsey (who coined the term 'cyberbullying'), which provides information, educational and training resources with the aim of eliminating bullying.

ChatDanger

www.chatdanger.com

This site provides advice about the potential dangers of online interactive services like chat, IM, online games, email and those on mobile phones.

CyberBully.org

www.cyberbully.org

Cyberbully.org is produced by the US Center for Safe and Responsible Internet Use, which provides resources for educators and parents to promote the safe and responsible use of the internet.

CyberSafeKids

www.cybersafekids.com.au

A useful site by Australian cyber-educator Robyn Treyvaud, where you will find regularly updated news, online resources for internet safety and cyberbullying, activities for children in safe environments, parent information and school resources.

Cybersmart Kids Online

www.cybersmartkids.com.au

This is a community awareness project developed by the Australian Communications and Media Authority with the objective of providing parents and children with information and tools to help them have a rewarding, productive and safe experience of the internet. It's a young person's guide to smart surfing, chatting and emailing. Parents can learn useful tips on safe ways to enjoy the best of the internet while protecting children from the worst. Teachers can use the lesson plan, online teaching resources and homework tips to help kids be cybersmart.

Family Online Safety Institute

www.icra.org/kids/familycontract

This is the sample Family Online Internet Safety Contract I included in chapter 8, developed by the Internet Content Rating Association (ICRA), part of the independent, international organisation Family Online Safety Institute.

GetNetWise

www.getnetwise.org

GetNetWise, produced by internet industry corporations and public interest organisations, seeks to provide the resources needed to make informed decisions about family use of the internet.

i-SAFE

www.iSafe.org

US organisation i-SAFE is a non-profit foundation dedicated to protecting the online experiences of youth everywhere, through school curriculum and community outreach programs.

Microsoft Security at Home

www.microsoft.com/security/protect/

The Microsoft Security at Home site provides advice for everyday users and beginners to improve the security of their home computers, and to help protect your family from inappropriate content and contact, viruses, identity theft and more.

NetAlert

www.netalert.net.au

The site of Australia's internet safety advisory body offers practical advice on internet safety, and parental control and filters for the protection of children, students and families. Read more about the risks for children online, such as chatting online, cyberbullying, online predators or online scams, and find solutions to these problems and more. NetAlert have also devised free online internet safety educational programs for kids of different age groups: www.nettysworld.com.au for ages 2–7, www.cyberquoll.com.au for ages 8–11, and www.cybernetrix.com.au for ages 12–18.

NetFamilyNews

www.netfamilynews.org

This is a non-profit forum for parents and educators in more than fifty countries, and includes a weekly email newsletter and daily blog distributed in partnership with SafeKids.com and London-based Childnet International.

Net-Mom's Internet Safe House

www.netmom.com

A US site by Jean Armour Polly, author of *Net-mom's Internet Kids & Family Yellow Pages*, a directory of 3500 of the best children's resources on the net.

NetSafe

www.netsafe.org.nz

This is the website of the Internet Safety Group of New Zealand, offering cybersafety education for children, parents, schools, community organisations and businesses. The ISG has been designated the NZ Ministry of Education's 'agent of choice' for cybersafety education in New Zealand. The site includes brilliant policies for schools.

NetSmartz Workshop
www.netsmartz.org
The NetSmartz Workshop is an interactive, educational safety resource for children aged 5–17, parents, guardians and educators. It uses age-appropriate, 3-D activities to teach children how to stay safe on the internet.

Online Child Sex Exploitation Team, Australian Federal Police
www.afp.gov.au/business/reporting_crime/reporting_national_crime/online_child_sex_exploitation
You can report any suspicious behaviour relating to pornography, abuse, or the grooming and procurement of children directly to the Australian Federal Police (AFP), through its Online Child Sex Exploitation Team (OCSET), on (07) 5553 8709 or email national-ocset-omc@afp.gov.au. Alternatively, the webpage has online reporting forms.

Safetynet

www.sofweb.vic.edu.au/internet/safety.htm

Safetynet: Internet Usage – Guidelines for Schools, is published by Victoria's Department of Employment, Education and Training, and includes a list of existing school cybersafety policies, which may assist parents to understand the principles of these agreements and to know what to look for from their child's school.

StopTextBully.com

www.stoptextbully.com

This accessible site advises children, and their parents and teachers, about how to deal with text abuse and threats, either via mobile phones or email and the web. Although geared primarily towards children it includes a section for parents.

WebsafeCrackerz

www.websafecrackerz.com

This US internet safety site was designed by teens for teens to help them understand the importance of safe surfing on the net.

It is an interactive site that asks young users what they should do in certain situations, requiring practical thinking and immediate action, and it mirrors many of the dangers that children face.

WiredSafety

www.wiredsafety.org

WiredSafety provides help, information and education to internet and mobile device users of all ages. It offers help to victims of cyber-abuse ranging from online fraud, cyberstalking and child safety, to hacking and malicious code attacks. It also offers help to parents with issues such as cyberbullying and the use of MySpace.

Index

acceptable use agreement 139, 140–1, 143
addiction to the internet
    does it exist? 66, 121, 132–3
    how much is too much? 131–2
    online gaming 65, 66, 125–6
    prevalence 123
    when substitute for human interaction 124–5, 131, 134
    and sleep deprivation 126–8
    what parents should do about 132–3
advertising and marketing 33, 53, 77, 78
Apple iPhone 52
auction sites 77
Australian Communications and Media Authority 80, 175
Australian Federal Police 78–9, 181–2
avatars 6, 49
BearShare 57
Belsey, Bill 92, 176
BitTorrent 57
blog (weblog) 8
broadband access to the net 3
browsers 4
browsing the web 4–5
buddies 6, 33
bullying *see* cyberbullying
caller-ID block 107
Campbell, Marilyn 97–8
censorware 52
Centre for Online Addiction 122
chat
    concealing true identity 7

    for instant message exchanges 6
    multiparticipant 6, 33
    nothing said can be retracted 35
    potential for cyberbullying 62
    saving bullying messages 35
    throwaway communication 34
ChatAlert! 109
Chatblocker 109
chatrooms
    bullying 97
    chatting to strangers 34
    microphone connection 6–7
    online meeting places 6, 33–4
    webcams 7
ClubPenguin 50, 64
Columbine High School massacre 95
Coonan, Helen 73
credit card billing 55
cyberbullying 38, 72–4, 76
    Alex Teka 89–91
    blocking the bullies 106–7
    combating 102–5
    and disinhibition 92–3
    girls more likely victims 98–9
    'griefers' 62
    'happy slapping' 72, 96
    if your child is a bully 114–18
    if your child is a victim 106–9
    outside school hours 143
    physical threats 108
    picture/video clip bullying 96
    'pranking' 115
    prevalence 97–9
    protective software 109
    reporting 107–8

saving the evidence 35, 108
signs of 99–101
tracking down 93–4
types of 95–7
what is it? 92–5
what parents should do about
    102–5, 114–19
Cyberbullying.org website 100–1, 103,
    108, 176
Cyberia 11, 13, 43, 84
cybersafety *see* safety contract; safety
    principles; schools and cybersafety
dangers of internet 71
    financial risks 76–7
    identity theft 77–8
    inappropriate material 75
    predators and personal safety 74–5, 78
    what parents can do 78–87
    see also cyberbullying
dial-up access 3
digital generation gap 11–25
'digital natives' 12–14
disinhibition 92–3
downloading
    credit card billing 55
    free 56, 58–60
    illegal 56, 57
    what parents should do 57
email (electronic mail) 2
    address unique to user 5
    attaching files 5–6
    bullying 97
    chat 6–7
    different accounts for different
        purposes 6
    exchanging written messages 5
    free accounts 6
    queued in a mailbox 5
    stored until deleted 34
eMailTrackerPro 109

emoticons 34
ENUFF 23, 67–8
Facebook social network site 8
Family Online Internet Safety Contract
    see safety contract
filters
    all families should use 54
    best filter between child's ears 52–3,
        83–4
    censorware 52
    circumventing 52, 82–3
    covert 81
    in libraries 82
    ISP 54, 82
    National Filter Scheme 73, 82, 83
    none for mobile phones 52
    in schools 83, 142
financial risks 76–7
Firefox browser 4
forums 7
free downloads 56, 58–60
Fuller, Andrew 127
gaming online
    addiction to 65, 66, 125–6
    age to start playing 64–5
    classifying games 60–1, 66
    educational games 64
    MMORPGs 61–3, 125
    parents' attitudes to 63
    software to limit time 67
    time limits 65–6, 67–8
    what parents should do about it 65,
        66–8
Goldberg, Dr Ivan 122
Google search engine 4–5
Greenfield, Dr David 133
'griefers' 62
'happy slapping' 72, 96
Hotmail 6
identity, concealing 5, 7, 8

identity theft 77–8
illegal downloading 56, 57
IM (instant messaging) 6, 32, 33, 97, 106
inappropriate material 38, 75
internet
    access to 3
    addiction to 66, 121–35
    common use to upload 3
    dangers of 71–87
    how much is too much 131–2, 134
    legal ramifications of activity 35,
        37–8, 48, 51
    making it a family activity 24
    penalties for net-abuse 170–1
    portability of 16
    in public places 3
    rules for use 17–18, 25, 38, 126–7
    services 4–8
    statistics of child use 12–13
    switching off for sleep 126–7
    unsupervised use 19
    what is it? 2–4
    what parents should do about it
        24–5, 37–8
    why it is a problem 15–17
Internet Addiction Disorder 122
Internet Explorer browser 4
Internet Service Provider (ISP) 2, 5,
    54, 82
i-SAFE advice 38, 46–7, 56, 57, 66, 178–9
legal ramifications of online activity 35,
    37–8, 48, 51
libraries and filters 82
Limewire 57
mailbox 5
McLean, Senior Constable Susan 65, 71
meeting strangers 18, 30, 37, 51, 67,
    173, 155
microphone connection 6–7
MMORPG (Massively Multiplayer

Online Role-Playing Games) 61–3,
    125
mobile phones
    for bullying 96
    caller-ID block 107
    internet-enabled 3, 139, 141
    no filtering software for 52
    ownership statistics 139
    SMS most common function 35
MSN (Windows Live Messenger) 32, 33
Mubarak Ali, Dr Rahamatulla 123–4
MySpace social networking site 7, 8,
    28, 42–3, 43–4, 46, 83
National Filter Scheme 73, 82, 83
Neal, Jack 13–14
net-abuse penalties 170–1
NetAlert (safety advisory body) 17–18, 24,
    78–9, 82, 99, 108, 126, 131–2, 179–80
netiquette 38, 104
Netscape browser 4, 144
Nickelodeon 64
OCSET (Online Child Sex Exploitation
    Team) 78–9, 181–2
offensive material, reporting 80
Opera browser 4
Orzack, Dr Maressa 125
parents
    digital generation gap 11–25
    educating 80–1
    Family Online Internet Safety
        Contract 160–1
    getting involved in kids' online lives
        23–4
    perceptions of the internet 13
    sharing passwords 37
    spying on online activities 45, 46
    told about inappropriate encounters
        38
    understanding virtual world bullying
        137

what to say to your kids 167–74
why the internet is a problem 15–17
parental control software 25, 135
passwords, not sharing 30–1, 37, 103
Paulson, Amanda 102
PayPal 55
personal details not given online 29, 37,
    50–1, 67, 154, 155
'phishing' 76
photos posted 48, 50
picture/video clip bullying 96
police, contacting 78, 108
pop-up advertising 53, 54
'pranking' 115
predators and personal safety 74–5, 78
Prensky, Marc 12
Roberts, Jane 53
Roennebeg, Professor Till 127
rules for use 17–18, 25, 38, 126–7
    making before issues arise 31
RuneScape 63, 64
Safari browser 4
safety contract 25
    agreement in writing 152–3
    awareness of predators 157
    behaviour online away from home
    158
    bullying prohibited and reported 156
    child's contract 161–3
    currencies (rewards) 152
    distressing material reported 156–7
    downloading guidelines 57
    emails from unknowns not opened
    156
    fiscal responsibility 157
    formalising family's use 149–50
    no chatroom without permission 155
    no completing forms 155
    no details of real life 154, 155
    no meeting people in real life 155

parent contract 160–1
parents' right to supervise 158
public versus private information 158
signed by whole family 152, 158–9
social networking contacts limited
    155–6
time limits agreed and enforced 31,
    38, 153, 157
safety principles
    downloading guidelines 57
    file-sharing dangers 56, 57
    legal ramifications 35, 37–8, 48, 51
    no access to credit cards 55
    no meeting strangers 30, 37, 51,
    67, 173
    no opening messages from unknown
    senders 104
    no personal details or photos 29,
    37, 50–1, 67, 103, 172–3
    no response to inappropriate emails
    38
    no sharing passwords 30–1, 37, 103
    on signs of bullying 102–5
    social network sites to be private 50
    time limits agreed and enforced 31,
    38
    see also filters
scams 76, 77–8
schools and cybersafety
    acceptable use agreement 139,
    140–1, 143
    cybersafety agreement 144–5
    dealing with bullying 107, 142–3
    filtering software 83, 142
    net-enabled items brought on site
    141–2, 146
    what parents should do 146–7
    what should parents expect 140–3
    when rules are broken 143–4
screen name 29, 43

search engines 4–5
Second Life virtual community 49
sexual exploitation, protecting your child 78–9
sleep deprivation 126–8
SMS 35, 36, 96
social networking
    dangers of exposing details 7–8
    list of friends 8, 44
    no meetings 51
    parents should see site 45–6
    photographs posted 8, 49, 50
    possibilities for bullying 97
    privacy settings 43–4, 47, 50
    public sites 43
    risks 8
    screen name 43
    blogs 8
    site content filtered 44
    true identity can be concealed 8
    use by younger children 44
    virtual communities 49
software
    enables parents to spy 46, 58–60
    parental control software 25, 135
    protects against bullying 109
spam 54, 78
subscription services 77
sunk cost fallacy 126
surfing the web 3, 5
    commercial messages 51–2, 53
    filtering software 52
    what parents should do about 53–4
Surviving Adolescents 124
Teen Second Life virtual community 49
text messages *see* SMS
The Princess Bitchface Syndrome 35
time limits
    agreed and enforced 31, 38, 153, 157

    on gaming 65–6, 67–8
Treyvaud, Robyn 8
usernames 29
virtual communities 49
viruses 56
web 2–3
web browsing and searching 4–5
    checking sites visited 54
webcams 7
weblog (blog) 8
websites
    accessed via browser 4
    addresses 4
    bullying via 97
    links 3
    search engines find unknown addresses 4
Werribee 'happy slapping' case 72–4, 96
Whyvillenet (younger users) 50
Windows Live Messenger 32, 33
wireless access to the net 3, 19
World of Warcraft 62, 64
World Wide Web *see* web
worms 56
Xanga social network site 7, 47
Young, Kimberly 122, 132
younger children
    checking social networking 44
    filters for 84
    games aimed at 64
    including in safety contract 150
    learning online behaviour 13–14, 53
    no gaming 67
    no internet access in their rooms 52
    protected sites for 50
    social networking 44, 50
YouTube 72–3, 74, 79, 83, 138, 142